A
Black Country
Christmas

A
Black Country
Christmas

Compiled by Robin Pearson

ALAN SUTTON

First published in the United Kingdom in 1992
Alan Sutton Publishing Limited · Phoenix Mill · Far Thrupp
Stroud · Gloucestershire

First published in the United States of America in 1993
Alan Sutton Publishing Inc · Wolfeboro Falls
NH 03896–0848

British Library Cataloguing in Publication Data

Black Country Christmas
I. Pearson, Robin
820.8033

ISBN 0-7509-0071-7

Library of Congress Cataloging in Publication Data applied
for

Cover illustration: Arriving at the Inn, *anon (Fine Art
Photographs Ltd)*

Typeset in Garamond 12/13.
Typesetting and origination by
Alan Sutton Publishing Limited.
Printed in Great Britain by
The Bath Press, Avon.

Contents

v

Christmas Cheer in the Black Country

FREDERICK W. HACKWOOD

*A prolific recorder of local customs and superstitions,
Wednesbury's Frederick Hackwood was the author of many a
history of individual Black Country towns. Here in his* Sedgley
Researches, *published in 1898, he describe some of the region's
Christmas traditions.*

Carol Singing – The practice of the 'carol singers' in the Black
County is for them to wait until the bells have ended their
'merry midnight peal' before they sally forth, and then to
commence their carols at the houses of those most likely to
bestow 'largess' in honour of the season. Some time people sit
up to receive them, and treat them liberally with 'cakes and
ale'. Generally, however, after singing a carol the 'waits' pass
on, and call again for the customary donation when the household is astir next day preparing for the Christmas dinner.

Christmas customs do not vary much over very wide areas,
and certainly scarcely at all over the whole of the Black
Country region. The preparations at Sedgley, Wednesbury,
and all the adjacent parishes generally include the killing of a
pig – the specially 'fatted' pig – and the making of pork pies
and pig's puddings. Most well-to-do artisans feed their own
pigs, and their pig-killing takes place a week or two before

Taking the holly and presents home three days before Christmas
1970 on Langley High Street

Christmas. More immediately before Christmas the good housewife busies herself in making mince pies and plum puddings and getting ready other 'Christmas cheer'.

'Christmas cheer' in the Black Country is a proverbial expression, and something more. No one who has passed through the district when the Christmas show of meat, game, and poultry was on view would for a moment doubt either the loyalty of the people of King Christmas, or the faith of the caterers in the appetites of the population. Eating and drinking are, for the nonce, the serious occupations of nearly everybody. Indigestion, with its complement the blue pill, has no terrors for the miner and mechanic, the iron worker and the labourer.

Two years later Hackwood published his Religious Wednesbury *which contains this reference to the festive generosity of a nearby clergyman.*

One seldom mentioned was a custom in the neighbouring parish of Great Barr, on Christmas Day, where the rector gave to each person, great and small, of his parish, who chose to come to his house for the same, as much bread, beef, mustard, and vinegar as he could eat. The edibles have been discontinued, but money is sometimes given now instead.

Fire and Snow

CHARLES DICKENS

Readings by the great Victorian novelist proved so popular in Wolverhampton that Charles Dickens was prompted to describe audiences there as 'wonderful', particularly after their reception of a rendering of A Christmas Carol *in 1858. In the magazine* Household Words *he recounts his first wintry visit to the town five years earlier.*

Can this be the region of cinders and coaldust, which we have traversed before now, divers times, both by night and by day, when the dirty wind rattled as it came against us charged with fine particles of coal, and the natural colour of the earth and all its vegetation might have been black, for anything our eyes could see to the contrary in a waste of many miles? Indeed it is the same country, though so altered that on this present day when the old year is near its last, the North East wind blows white, and all the ground is white – pure white – insomuch that if our lives depended on our identifying a mound of ashes as we jar along this Birmingham and Wolverhampton Railway, we could not find a handful.

The sun shines brightly, though it is a cold cold sun, this piercing day; and when the Birmingham tunnel disgorges us into the frosty air, we find the pointsman housed in no mere box, but in a resplendent pavilion, all bejewelled with dazzling icicles, the least a yard long. A radiant pointsman he should be, we think, invested by fairies with a dress of

rainbow hues, and going round and round in some gorgeously playful manner on a gold and silver pivot. But, he has changed neither his stout great coat, nor his stiff hat, nor his stiff attitude of watch; and as (like the ghostly dagger of Macbeth) he marshals us the way that we were going, we observe him to be a mortal with a red face – red, in part from a seasonable joviality of spirit, and in part from frost and wind – with the encrusted snow dropping silently off his out-stretched arm.

Redder than ever are the very red-brick little houses outside Birmingham – all staring at the railway in the snowy weather, like plethoric old men with white heads. Clean linen drying in yards seems ill-washed, against the intense white of the landscape. Far and near, the tall tall chimneys look out over one another's shoulders for the swart ashes familiar to them, and can discern nothing but snow. Is this the smoke of other chimneys setting in so heavily from the north-east, and overclouding the short brightness of the day? No. By the North Pole it is more snow!

Making directly at us, and flying almost horizontally before the wind, it rushes against the train, in a dark blast profusely speckled as it were with drifting white feathers. A sharp collision, though a harmless one! No wonder that the engine seems to have a fearful cold in his head. No wonder, with a deal of out-door work in such a winter, that he is very hoarse and very short of breath, very much blown when we come to the next station, and very much given to weeping, snorting and spitting, all the time he stops!

Which is short enough, for these little upstairs stations at the tops of high arches, whence we almost look down the chimneys of scattered workshops, and quite inhale their smoke as it comes puffing at us – these little upstairs stations rarely seem to do much business anywhere, and just now are like suicidal heights to dive from into depths of snow. So,

away again over the moor, where the clanking serpents usually writhing above coal-pits, are dormant and whitened over – this being holiday time – but where those grave monsters, the blast-furnaces, which cannot stoop to recreation, are awake and roaring. Now, a smoky village; now, a chimney; now, a dormant serpent who seems to have been benumbed in the act of working his way for shelter into the lonely little engine-house by the pit's mouth; now, a pond with black specks sliding and skating; now, a drift with similar specks half sunken in it throwing snowballs; now, a cold white altar of snow with fire blazing on it; now, a dreary open space of mound and fell, snowed smoothly over, and closed in at last by sullen cities of chimneys. Not altogether agreeable to think of crossing such space without a guide, and being swallowed by a long-abandoned, long-forgotten shaft. Not even agreeable, in this undermined country, to think of half-a-dozen railway arches with the train upon them, suddenly vanishing through the snow into the excavated depths of a coal-forest.

Snow, wind, ice, and Wolverhampton – all together. No carriage at the station, everything snowed up. So much the better. The Swan will take us under its warm wing, walking or riding. Where is the Swan's nest? In the market-place. So much the better yet, for it is market-day, and there will be something to see from the Swan's nest.

Up the streets of Wolverhampton, where the doctor's bright door-plate is dimmed as if Old Winter's breath were on it, and the lawyer's office window is appropriately misty, to the market-place: where we find a cheerful bustle and plenty of people – for the most part pretending not to like the snow, but liking it very much, as people generally do. The Swan is a bird of a good substantial brood, worthy to be a country cousin of the hospitable Hen and Chickens, whose company we have deserted for only a few hours and with whom we shall roost again at Birmingham to-night. The Swan has bountiful

coal-country notions of firing, snug homely rooms, cheerful windows looking down upon the clusters of snowy umbrellas in the market-place, and on the chaffering and chattering which is pleasantly hushed by the thick white down lying so deep, and softly falling still. Neat bright-eyed waitresses do the honors of the Swan. The Swan is confident about its soup, is troubled with no distrust concerning cod-fish, speaks the word of promise in relation to an enormous chine of roast beef, one of the dishes at 'the Ironmasters' dinner,' which will be disengaged at four. The Ironmasters' dinner! It has an imposing sound. We think of the Ironmasters joking, drinking to their Ironmistresses, clinking their glasses with a metallic ring, and comporting themselves at the festive board with the might of men who have mastered Iron.

Now for a walk! Not in the direction of the furnaces, which we will see to-night when darkness shall set off the fires; but in the country, with our faces towards Wales. Say, ye hoary finger-posts whereon the name of picturesque old Shrewsbury is written in characters of frost; ye hedges lately bare, that have burst into snowy foliage; ye glittering trees from which the wind blows sparkling dust; ye high drifts by the roadside, which are blue a-top, where ye are seen opposed to the bright red and yellow of the horizon; say all of ye, is summer the only season for enjoyable walks! Answer, roguish crow, alighting on a sheep's back to pluck his wool off for an extra blanket, and skimming away, so black, over the white field; give us your opinion, swinging ale-house signs, and cosey little bars; speak out, farrier's shed with faces all a-glow, fountain of sparks, heaving bellows, and ringing music; tell us, cottage hearths and sprigs of holly in cottage windows; be eloquent in praise of wintry walks, you sudden blasts of wind that pass like shiverings of Nature, you deep roads, you solid fragments of old hayricks with your fragrance frozen in! Even you, drivers of toiling carts, coal-laden, keeping company together

'The Swan will take us under its warm wing.' The pub (with its portico in the centre of this photograph) looked down on the Market Place – today's Queen Square where a bank now occupies the site – of Dickens' refuge from 'snow, wind and ice'

behind your charges, dog-attended and basket-bearing: even you though it is no easy work to stop, every now and then, and chip the snow away from the clogged wheels with picks, will have a fair word to say for winter, will you not!

Down to the solitary factory in the dip of the road, deserted of holiday-makers, and where the water-mill is frozen up – then turn. As we draw nigh to our bright bird again, the early evening is closing in, the cold increases, the snow deadens and darkens, and lights spring up in the shops. A wet walk, ankle deep in snow the whole way. We must buy some stockings, and borrow the Swan's slippers before dinner.

It is a mercy that we step into the toy-shop to buy a pocket-comb too, or the pretty child-customer (as it seems to us,

the only other customer the elderly lady of the toy-shop has lately had), might have stood divided between the two puzzles at one shilling each, until the putting up of the shutters. But, the incursion of our fiery faces and snowy dresses, coupled with our own individual recommendation of the puzzle on the right hand, happily turn the scale. The best of pocket-combs for a shilling, and now for the stockings. Dibbs 'don't keep 'em', though he writes up that he does, and Jibbs is so beleaguered by country people making market-day and Christmas-week purchases, that his shop is choked to the pavement. Mibbs is the man for our money, and Mibbs keeps everything in the stocking line, though he may not exactly know where to find it. However, he finds what we want, in an inaccessible place, after going up ladders for it like a lamp-lighter; and a very good article it is, and a very civil worthy trader Mibbs is, and may Mibbs increase and multiply! Likewise young Mibbs, unacquainted with the price of anything in stock, and young Mibbs's aunt who attends to the ladies' department.

The Swan is rich in slippers – in those good old flip-flap inn slippers which nobody can keep on, which knock double knocks on every stair as their wearer comes down stairs, and fly away over the banisters before they have brought him to level ground. Rich also is the Swan in wholesome well-cooked dinner, and in tender chine of beef, so brave in size that the mining of all the powerful Ironmasters is but a sufficient outlet for its gravy. Rich in things wholesome and sound and unpretending is the Swan, except that we would recommend the good bird not to dip its beak into its sherry. Under the change from snow and wind to hot soup, drawn red curtains, fire and candle, we observe our demonstrations at first to be very like the engine's at the little station; but they subside, and we dine vigorously – another tribute to a winter walk! – and finding that the Swan's ideas of something hot to drink

are just and laudable, we adopt the same, with emendations (in the matter of lemon chiefly) of which modesty and total abstinence principles forbid the record. Then, thinking drowsily and delightfully of all things that have occurred to us during the last four-and-twenty hours, and of most things that have occurred to us during the last four-and-twenty years, we sit in arm chairs, amiably basking before the fire – playthings for infancy – creatures to be asked a favour of – until aroused by the fragrance of hot tea and muffins. These we have ordered, principally as a perfume.

The bill of the Swan is to be commended as not out of pro-portion to its plumage; and now, our walking shoes being dried and baked, we must get them on somehow – for the rosy driver with his carriage and pair who is to take us among the fires on the blasted heath by Bilston announces from under a few shawls, and the collars of three or four coats, that we must be going. Away we go, obedient to the summons, and, having taken leave of the lady in the Swan's bar opposite the door, who is almost rustled out of her glass case and blown

Snow-topped carriages line up at Chapel Ash

upstairs whenever the door opens, we are presently in outer darkness grinding the snow.

Soon the fires begin to appear. In all this ashy country, there is still not a cinder visible; in all this land of smoke, not a stain upon the universal white. A very novel and curious sight is presented by the hundreds of great fires blazing in the midst of the cold dead snow. They illuminate it very little. Sometimes, the construction of a furnace, kiln, or chimney, admits of a tinge being thrown upon the pale ground near it; but, generally the fire burns in its own sullen ferocity, and the snow lies impassive and untouched. There is a glare in the sky, flickering, now, and then, over the greater furnaces, but the earth lies stiff in its winding sheet and the huge corpse candles burning above it affect it no more than colossal tapers of state move dead humanity.

Sacrificial altars, varying in size, but all gigantic, and all made of ice and snow, abound. Tongues of flame shoot up from them, and pillars of fire turn and twist upon them. Fortresses on fire, a whole town in a blaze, Moscow newly kindled, we see fifty times; rattling and crashing noises strike the ear, and the wind is loud. Thus, crushing the snow with our wheels, and sidling over hillocks of it, and sinking into drifts of it, we roll on softly through a forest of conflagration; the rosy-faced driver, concerned for the honor of his locality, much regretting that many fires are making holiday to-night, and that we see so few.

Come we at last to the precipitous wooden steps by which we are to be mast-headed at a railway station. Good night to rosy-face, the cheeriest man we know, and up. Station very gritty, as a general characteristic. Station very dark, the gas being frozen. Station very cold, as any timber cabin suspended in the air with such a wind making lunges at it, would be. Station very dreary, being a station. Man and boy behind money-taking partition, checking accounts, and not able to

unravel a knot of seven and sixpence. Small boy, with a large package on his back, like Christian with his bundle of sins, sent down into the snow an indefinite depth and distance, with instructions to 'look sharp in delivering that, and then cut away back here for another'. Second small boy in search of basket for Mr Brown, unable to believe that it is not there, and that anybody can have dared to disappoint Brown. Six third-class passengers prowling about, and trying in the dim light of one oil lamp to read with interest the dismal time-bills and notices about throwing stones at trains, upon the walls. Two more, scorching themselves at the rusty stove. Shivering porter going in and out, bell in hand, to look for the train, which is overdue, finally gives it up for the present, and puts down the bell – also the spirits of the passengers. In our own innocence we repeatedly mistake the roaring of the nearest furnace for the approach of the train, run out, and return covered with ignominy. Train in sight at last – but the other train – which don't stop here – and it seems to tear the trembling station limb from limb, as it rushes through. Finally, some half-an-hour behind its time through the tussle it has had with the snow, comes our expected engine, shriek-ing with indignation and grief. And as we pull the clean white coverlet over us in bed at Birmingham, we think of the whiteness lying on the broad landscape all around for many a frosty windy mile, and find that it makes bed very comfort-able.

Winter

LUKE BOOKER

Dudley's early nineteenth-century vicar, Luke Booker, was also a poet. His first published work was the two-volume, Poems on subjects sacred, moral and entertaining, *from which this extract is taken. He was much in demand as a charity preacher, raising £9,000 from 173 sermons. Booker is also noteworthy for composing the epitaph for Sutton Coldfield murder victim May Ashford and for writing a pamphlet refuting the defence case of her alleged killer, Abraham Thornton, at his first trial.*

From regions of eternal snow,
Lo! hoary Winter seeks our land;
The mountain high – the valley low,
Alike declare his icy hand.

In shining fetters bound, the stream
No murmur lends to sooth the ear;
No warmth conveys the noon-tide beam,
Creation's torpid works to cheer.

No flow'r adorns the wasted plain,
Nor plants' fair verdure decks the lawn:
Grey mists usurp the wide domain,
And robe, with down, each tree and thorn.

The timid hare, from home to stray,
O'er woodland wild in search of fare
(Lest she her vestiges betray)
Kind instinct whispers to forbear.

Where sung the lark its matin strains,
The wint'ry fieldfare now is seen;
And dazzling snow makes white those plains
Which once were dress'd in lovelier green. –

Thus diff'rent, Sylvia, things appear;
In nature's scale ordain'd to move: –
Throughout the ever-rolling year,
The Seasons change – but not my love.

from

Ruffy and Sons

GEORGE WODEN

*George Wilson Slaney, born in Wednesbury and educated at
Walsall's Queen Mary Grammar School, 'abandoned' his career
as an engineer to become a journalist and later a schoolmaster
in Glasgow. He did not forget his connections with his native
'tube town' as he wrote under the appropriate pseudonym of
George Woden. Wednesbury had its origins in pagan Saxon*

*times as 'Woden's burh' (fort). Its modern nickname came from
the prosperity brought about by the revolutionary methods of
butt welding in tube production by Cornelius Whitehouse.
Although not mentioned in this extract, Slaney included him in
this novel to give it historical background and 'also in tribute to
a neglected genius'.*

Winter approached, stripping the trees to cold skeletons, lashing the countryside with rain, the sun on quiet days flushed red in mist, and setting in fiery splendour on stormy afternoons, the moon, riding through the tempestuous breakers of the clouds, shining on the wet roofs as on burnished steel. One morning John looked out of the window, and, like every other youngster, rejoiced to see the white magic of snow; and he trotted to school through a dancing mist of flakes. Old folk remembered similar early winters, years ago, and shook their heads prophetically. In the Jubilee Park there were snow cushions on roses and chrysanthemums; and when the sun melted the snow the shadows under the bushes were white and the sunny patches black and glistening. But nobody walked in the park to see this unusual beauty. Old Mr Pincock and his gardeners saw only the sodden dahlias and the work to be done.

Peter Rowley announced in the gossip column of the *Advertiser* that Mr Humblewade, of Ladypool, had gone to Africa to shoot big game. So Humblewade had not proposed to Lucy Ruffy. Or had he not been accepted? Mr Bernard Ruffy was to spend the winter in the Mediterranean for his health. Lucky rascal, gambling away his father's money at Monte Carlo, no doubt. John Ruffy's daughter, Mary, sighed at the thought; for her own child Margaret, poor wee soul, coughed and coughed, even in her sleep through the night. The doctor's bottles didn't cure her, nor even the concoction from the herbalist – horehound, hyssop, aniseed, polypody

root, ginger, liquorice – a cure guaranteed by the old man himself, who sold bottles every winter to the same faithful sufferers. John, nicknamed Scottie, in a woollen tam-o'shanter and a huge knitted muffler, was envied by all his playmates. He loved to see the garden path risen like a baking loaf, the stones lying heavy in the holes. Cold fluffy sparrows were magnified in fog to the size of starlings, and starlings to crows. The mud accumulated on doorscraper and mat, and the dirt everywhere.

Christmas came. The Market Place expanded to twice its normal size to hold all the turkeys and geese, the prize carcasses, the joints of meat and the festoons of sausages, the clothes and crockery, the quack doctors, the shows which overflowed from the fair ground behind the Saracen's Head, and the holly and mistletoe. Never was such a bustle, such flaring lights and intoxicating scents, such a glorious cacophony of music. John and wee Margaret were allowed to sit up on Christmas Eve, as they had in Scotland on Hogmanay to let the New Year in, to hear the bells, and to join in the

Wednesbury Market Place in the 1890s

chorus with the singers in the fine old carol, 'As I sat on a sunny bank'. Old Mr Rowley arrived, by the front door, and John, peeping into the room, saw a parcel which had not been there before. Solemnly Mr Rowley fixed short branches from an elder tree above the children's beds, and went outside again to draw a magic chalk mark and crosses before the house, to keep away all elves, goblins, witches and warlocks, during the holy time. 'This is what our forefathers did, long ago,' he explained. And the children understood that old Mr Rowley must be very old indeed.

A Christmas Rhyme for Children

DAVID BAILEY

Although born in Sedgley David Bailey was clearly associated with Bilston, where he and his wife, both described as born teachers, opened schools. His 1859 pamphlet The Truck System *was believed to have been instrumental in ending the 'Tommy Shop' payments for workers. Apart from poetry his other great interest was spelling, which prompted him to write two books on phonetics – testimony to his life-long friendship with shorthand inventor Sir Isaac Pitman.*

To celebrate the Saviour's birth,
The bells of heaven were rung on earth,
And happy angels lowly bent
To herald forth the great event;
Redeeming Love had come to men,
To win them back to God again.

'Twas in the night time they appeared,
The simple shepherds greatly feared,
For round them, with celestial light,
The glory of the Lord shone bright;
And as they humbly bowed the head,
An angel standing by them said:

'Fear not, for Christ the Lord is born,
The Saviour of a world forlorn,
In David's town, of David's line,
And this shall be to you a sign: –
The babe, in swaddling clothes arrayed,
Is in a camel's manger laid.'

Then multitudes of angels sang,
The sky with hallelujahs rang;
'Glory to God,' the anthem ran,
'On earth be peace, good will to man';
Oh! sweet, and glad, and full of love,
That music from the spheres above!

So when the angels went away,
The shepherds moved at break of day;
To Bethlehem with haste they drew,
And proved the glorious tidings true;
Then wide abroad they made well known
The things which God to them had shown.

And aged Simeon, Anna too,
Beheld the Christ with grateful view,
And by the Spirit they declared
That God redemption had prepared;
A Light He was to every nation,
That all in Him might find salvation.

There came wise men from distant lands,
With costly treasures in their hands;
On Jesus Christ they would confer
Gold, frankincense, and wholesome myrrh;
Led by a star, the King they found,
And worshipped, falling to the ground.

By learning what the wise men knew,
And saying he would worship too,
The wily Herod sought to slay
The Lord's Anointed from his way;
But God revealed the horrid thought,
And Christ was into Egypt brought.

But still the wicked king defied
The providence of God, and tried
By slaughter to entrap the Child,
And oh! the wail of mothers wild!
Each male of two years old and under,
His soldiers' swords did cut asunder.

But Jesus grew a favoured boy,
A friend to all, His mother's joy;
His Father's house He early sought,
And often in the temple taught;
He never once went wrong or rude,
But spent His life in doing good.

And now our Christmas chant is sung,
In simple strains to suit the young;
But older people, if they choose,
May think, as they these lines peruse,
How wonderful was God's descent,
What love the condescension meant!

from

Weather Bound

RUPERT TURBERVILLE SMITH

'The weather is a great beginner of conversations,' wrote the compiler of twenty-seven years of records taken from observation stations in Dudley, Rowley Regis, Tettenhall and West Bromwich. In 1900 Rupert Turberville Smith felt meteorology should be taught in schools and that his readers should 'be able to return less inane replies than common to the frequent topic of weather'. Here he records the weather in December 1874.

December 5. Brisk rise of barometer at 8 a.m. Wind veered to W. and increasing to fresh breeze.
December 8. Barometer fell steadily all day, wind 7–8, S.E. to S. and rain. Barometer at 11 p.m. 28.132, reduced 28.622.
December 9. New moon at 0 hour 6 min. morning; it is said

the nearer the new moon is to midnight the more the effect for change of weather. The transit of Venus early in the morn of the 9th.

December 11.   Wind blowing 6 during the night. Barometer 28.072, reduced 28.566 at 5 p.m. on 11th, and only slightly higher at 11 p.m.

December 13.   Wind 6 all night, 10 increased to 7 with slight snow and sleet, 6 hours; wind 5.

December 18.   Skating on the Fenn's pool (Dudley) daily till 28th.

December 24.   Fall of snow in the night, and thaw afterwards.

December 28.   Fall of snow in the night.

A Very Dry and Warm Year in England.

The boating lake in West Smethwick Park froze over to provide a crowded opportunity for skating

A Capful O' Nails

DAVID CHRISTIE MURRAY

*West Bromwich born Murray led a fascinating life as a journalist
both locally and in London before becoming a war correspondent for*
The Scotsman *and* The Times *during the Russo–Turkish War
of 1877–8. The harsh realities of working life in the industries of
the Black Country can be found in some of his many books. When
he wrote* A Capful O' Nails *it was out of a sense of indignation at
the poor working conditions endured by nailmakers, and he did not
soften the text to make it 'more attractive as a work of art' when it
was published in 1896.*

They glistened like gold as he turned them over in his extend-
ed palm.

'Now, Salter, who's the best scholard here?'

Father named his most docile and obedient pupil.

'Then here's a bran'-new penny-piece for him,' said Mr
Jeremiah. 'An' who's the next best? This little feller? Then
here's a bran'-new penny-piece for him. An' who's the next
best?'

All the students got a penny each, and made as much of it
as if it were a sovereign.

'An' now, my b'ys,' said Mr Jeremiah, 'I shall do that for
ivery lad as comes here ivery night till Christmas – that is, for
them as is well reported on by the gaffer.'

We gave Mr Jeremiah three hearty cheers.

It is strange to think that the intrusion of this unharmful creature into our affairs should have orphaned me and left my mother a widow, and yet it happened so.

I have never blamed poor Mr Jeremiah, for, in any case, the storm would have broken upon us, and there were signs enough that it was brewing.

We were setting ourselves up to be better than our neighbours; we were making enmities between those neighbours and the foggers by whose good will they lived. My father had taken to wearing a shirt-collar; that's a curious thing to put in a fatal indictment – a count of life and death – and yet they put it there. My father's ill-spared bribe to each of his scholars, and Mr Jeremiah's pence, brought pupils still, but they came in defiance of their fathers and mothers, because they came against the countenance of the foggers; and the night-school bred dissension in many households. Angry men came and took away their sons, often enough with violence, and always with threats of violence.

Latterly, it came to pass that there was a nightly scene, and the roughs of the district – who were plentiful, Heaven knows! – hung about in anticipation of it, and enjoyed it hugely when it came.

I look back, and I think of it all with wonder, and yet with understanding. Here was a man who was spending his life in unremitting labour for the good of those about him – a man who, born in any other place in life, would have made for himself a name; a man of heart and brains; a man of courage, pity, and endurance – and every worthy faculty he had made him hateful to those for whom he laboured. He would have buttered their scanty bread for them, and have made it plentiful, if they would have allowed him to do it; but they thought he would rob them of what they had, and so, quite naturally, they hated him.

They had no courage to rise out of the slough they lay in, and they were angry with him because he had dared to do the thing which frightened them in the mere contemplation. Fierce, and ignorant, and hungry, bold in the mass, and cowardly when taken singly, they were no more to be civilized in a single generation than a pack of wolves.

God forbid that I should even seem to lump them all in one basket, for my father came of their stock, and many another good man, too, as I can well believe; but I speak of them in the mass, and I know that they were what the generations had made them.

On that last night Mr Allardyce was with us. I wish he had been anywhere else in the world, for he was not the sort of man one parts with lightly, or whose place in the world is

Lawyers Field, Wolverhampton, in the winter of 1955

24

soon filled. He came in smiling and cheerful, and shook hands with father and mother, and patted me on the head.

'And how's the night-school, Salter? I've come down to have another look at it, for I'm going into Hampshire tomorrow, to take the work of a friend of mine, and I may not be back for a month or more.'

'They're fallin' away, sir,' said father, with a kind of settled sadness. 'I've one lad left, and only one. They tek me for their enemy, poor things, an' they're all against our plans.'

'Never mind; courage and trust, Salter – courage and trust.'

'Ay, sir,' said father; 'the sum 'll work out all right in the end, no doubt. But we're only the figures in it; and, for my own part, sir, I feel as if I stood for nought without a figure before me.'

'We're all down-hearted at times,' said Mr Allardyce, lightly enough for him, who was commonly so serious. 'Shall we go?'

They went, and went to a grim ending, and I went with them, not because I was of any use to father's one big pupil, but because it had come to be a habit, and I did my own lessons at the night-school.

The road was pretty well alive in front of the cottage where Mr Brambler had hired the room for us, and Mr Allardyce was hustled, as well as father. It was done by apparent accident, but nobody was deceived by that. One fellow, a collier, if one might judge by the flannel clothes he wore, lurched heavily against the curate and staggered him. The man must have been there for the mere sport of the thing, for the colliers, at any rate, had no grudge against us.

'Have a little care, my friend,' said Mr Allardyce quite mildly, and somebody from behind knocked his silk hat clean over his eyes.

He freed himself from it and looked round, but the night was dark, and the nearest street-lamp was forty

yards away, so that he could make out nobody with any clearness.

'Will the man who did that show himself?' he asked. 'It isn't a very plucky thing to hit a man from behind, is it, boys?'

The only response was a 'boo-hoo!' of many voices from the outside edge of the crowd, and a rush which swayed the people who stood nearest against us.

'Better come in, sir,' said father. 'They'll be bent on mischief if we stop here.'

At the instant at which we entered the room and closed the door a brick was thrown, and broke into fragments on the wall of the house.

'What does all this mean, Salter?' asked Mr Allardyce. 'They cheered you in Barfield High Street only two months ago.'

'Not the nailers,' said father. 'There's plenty here only for sport tonight, but there's plenty more for mischief, and I wish you was safe at home, Mr Allardyce.'

'My dear Salter,' cried the curate, 'there's nothing to be afraid of. But you have no pupils here yet. I'm afraid that with this crowd outside there's little chance of school tonight.'

'Little chance, indeed, sir,' said father; and as he spoke the door opened.

'Here's your pupil,' said Mr Allardyce, and in came Mr Jeremiah, holding father's one pupil by the ear.

'This is a pretty sort of a rumpus, this is, Salter,' said he. 'I picked up this chap outside. I've paid him to come for his schoolin', an' now tonight he says he'll see me damned fust. So I just fetched him along, an' here he is.'

'There can be no school tonight', said Mr Allardyce, 'with this noise going on about us. I am afraid, Salter, that we shall have to abandon the scheme for a time. It will be more politic, perhaps. We can withdraw a little, to leap the better later on.'

'The night-school bred dissension in many households'

'You're not afeard o' this riff-raff, are you?' asked Mr
Jeremiah. 'I'll let 'em know who's who!'

There was a rising storm of hoots and groans outside, and
now and again a missile, hurled at hazard, struck the door. I
could scarcely hear what was said.

'Better let 'em quiet down,' said father.

'Leave 'em to me,' said Mr Jeremiah. He walked to the door
and opened it. 'Do you fellers know who I am?' he asked.

Somebody on the edge of the crowd bawled 'Mad Jerry!'
and there was a great shout of laughter.

'Let me get at that feller!' he cried, and as he moved forward something struck him on the shoulder. At this he hit
out at the man nearest to him, and in as little time as it takes

to tell it he was down. At the same second of time a stone crashed through the window and knocked over the solitary candle on the table. I saw all the rest dimly in the darkness, but father and Mr Allardyce charged out to rescue their companion, and in an instant, as it seemed, the whole mob was upon them. There was a mad welter and confusion, a shifting mass of figures, and nothing seen distinctly; but I heard the noise of blows, and a roar of oaths and curses, and I stood there shuddering and helpless in the darkness.

How long the *mêlée* lasted I cannot even guess. The fight was not all on one side, for I heard loud cries for fair play, and the thing lasted much too long to have been a mere struggle of two against three hundred. But shivering and crying bitterly in the darkness there, I heard that the confused noise grew fainter, and I saw the struggling figures fewer and fewer. The crowd seemed to break up and melt, and I heard a clattering of thick-booted feet upon the frozen wintry road. Then there came a dreadful silence, and I thought at first that the mob had carried father and Mr Allardyce away to work some mischief on them, for there was not a soul left in sight. But venturing from the door, I heard the crowd retreating in three directions – along the road on either side and down the lane in front.

I was frightened, as I had reason to be, and I called out for father as loudly as my shaking sobs would let me. Not a sound came in answer, and running blindly forward, I fell upon a prostrate figure. I explored it with my hands in a passion of terror.

'I didn't mek a Don at that job, nayther,' groaned poor Jerry Brambler.

He never spoke again.

I stood shrieking there, and not a living creature came near me. I tore my throat with cries. I besought Mr Jeremiah to tell me where father was, but he gave no sign.'

The night was dark as pitch, for some chance missile had smashed the glass of the only lamp in the street, and the wind had taken the light away from the burner.

I knelt on the icy ground and held for comfort to Mr Jeremiah's hand. It was warm when I first took it, and it seemed to give me a sort of courage, but it grew colder and colder and colder and colder, and at last it was so cold it frightened me.

I do not know who found me, or at what hour I was found, but I know that I awoke in the old home room, and that on the bed there lay a figure outlined under a rough sheet. That was all that was left of my father, who amongst his own class is remembered to this day in Quarrymoor and Castle Barfield as a man who deserted his class for gain.

Woodland setting for cottages and the Rose & Crown at Penn

The Carol of the Fir-Tree

ALFRED NOYES

Like his Bilston contemporary, Sir Henry Newbolt, Wolver-hampton poet Alfred Noyes was fond of the sea as a subject for his poetical compositions – Drake was their common factor. The fir-tree carol was published in the same year (1913) as two Christmas poems were privately printed in the United States where he had gone to take up a Princeton University professor-ship in modern English literature from 1914 to 1923.

Quoth the Fir-tree, 'Orange and vine'
Sing 'Nowell, Nowell, Nowell'!
'Have their honour: I have mine!'
In Excelsis Gloria!
'I am kin to the great king's house,'
Ring 'Nowell, Nowell, Nowell'!
And Lebanon whispers in my boughs.'
In Excelsis Gloria!

Apple and cherry, pear and plum,
Winds of Autumn, sigh 'Nowell'!
All the trees like mages come
Bending low with 'Gloria'!
Holding out on every hand
Summer pilgrims to Nowell!

Gorgeous gifts from Elfin-land.
And the May saith 'Gloria'!

Out of the darkness, who shall say –
Gold and myrrh for this Nowell! –
How they win their wizard way?
Out of the East with 'Gloria'!
Men that eat of the sun and dew,
Angels laugh and sing 'Nowell'
Call it 'fruit', and say it 'grew'!
Into the West with 'Gloria'!

'Leaves that fall,' whispered the Fir
Through the forest sing 'Nowell'!
'I am winter's minister.'
In Excelsis Gloria!
Summer friends may come and go,
Up the mountain sing 'Nowell'.
Love abides thro' storm and snow.
Down the valley, 'Gloria'!

'On my boughs, on mine, on mine,'
Father and mother, sing 'Nowell'!
'All the fruits of the earth shall twine.'
Bending low with 'Gloria'.
'Sword of wood and doll of wax'
Little children, sing 'Nowell'.
'Swing on the stem was cleft with the axe!'
Craftsmen all, a 'Gloria'.

'Hear! I have looked on the other side.'
Out of the East, O sing 'Nowell'!
'Because to live this night I died!'
Into the West with 'Gloria'.

'Hear! In this lighted room I have found'
Ye that seek, O sing 'Nowell'!
'The spell that worketh underground.'
Ye that doubt, a 'Gloria'.

'I have found it, even I,'
Ye that are lowly, sing 'Nowell'!
'The secret of this alchemy!'
Ye that are poor, a 'Gloria'.
'Look, your tinsel turneth to gold.'
Sing 'Nowell! Nowell! Nowell!'
'Your dust to a hand for love to hold!'
In Excelsis Gloria.

'Lay the axe at my young stem now!'
Woodman, woodman, sing 'Nowell'.
'Set a star on every bough!'
In Excelsis Gloria.
'Hall and cot shall see me stand,'
Rich and poor man, sing 'Nowell'!
'Giver of gifts from Elfin-land.'
Oberon, answer 'Gloria'.

'Hung by the hilt on your Christmas-tree'
Little children sing 'Nowell'!
'Your wooden sword is a cross for me.'
Emperors, a 'Gloria'.
'I have found that fabulous stone'
Ocean-worthies, cry 'Nowell'.
'Which turneth all things into one.'
Wise men all, a 'Gloria'.

'It is not ruby nor anything,' –
Jeweller, jeweller, sing 'Nowell'! –

'Fit for the crown of an earthly king.'
In Excelsis Gloria!
'It is not here! It is not there!'
Traveller, rest and cry 'Nowell'!
'It is one thing and everywhere!'
Heaven and Earth sing 'Gloria'.

'It is the earth, the moon, the sun,'
Mote in the sunbeam, sing 'Nowell'!
'And all the stars that march as one.'
In Excelsis Gloria!
'Here, by the touch of it, I can see'
Sing, O Life, a sweet Nowell!
'The world's King die on a Christmas-tree.'
Answer, Death, with 'Gloria'.

'Here, not set in a realm apart,'
East and West are one 'Nowell'!
'Holy Land is in your Heart!'
North and South one 'Gloria'!
'Death is a birth, birth is a death,'
Love is all, O sing 'Nowell'!
'And London one with Nazareth.'
And all the World a 'Gloria'.

'And angels over your heart's roof sing'
Birds of God, O pour 'Nowell'!
'That a poor man's son is the Son of a King!'
Out of your heart this 'Gloria'!
'Round the world you'll not away'
In your own soul, they sing 'Nowell'!
'From Holy Land this Christmas Day!'
In your own soul, this 'Gloria'.

from

Nurse on Call

EDITH COTTERILL

*Edith Cotterill has delighted her readers with tales of a Black
Country nurse. Having trained and become a nursing sister in
Kent, she later returned as a district nurse to her native Tipton,
which provided much material for her comical stories.*

Once more I was at Cotterill's Farm, the ancient home of my
father's family and once, for a short period of childhood, mine
too. Memories overwhelmed me: the mullioned windows; the
old priest-hole where we children played hide-and-seek;
Uncle Sim with his tight curly hair slicing mangel-wurzel
and surreptitiously slipping me a slice when Mother wasn't
looking. Sim, what a grand old family name, smacking of the
good earth and medieval husbandry. Sim, I rolled it round my
tongue and loved the flavour of it.

I recalled family Christmases, the roast turning endlessly
on the spit, carrots and peas on willow-pattern plates,
small boys in knickerbocker suits, hair smarmed back and
tongues in cheeks. Little girls with dodging on their drawers and fluted wings of broderie anglaise sprouting from
the shoulders of their starched white pinnys. Carols in the
parlour with the harsh horse-hair sofa scratching the back
of our bare legs, the aunts and uncles glorying in their
magnificent voices. Only Uncle George was inharmonious;

they shushed him and told him he would put a brass band out.

Then there was Big Jack with his powerful rendering of 'Danny Boy'. Many years later I was to hear him sing the haunting lament for the last time, on the day of his death, as he lay in the old fourposter in which they had all been born. This time it was in a tiny little voice but every note was true.

The farmhouse was a fine Tudor building with modern comforts and capable of housing three families. In 1638 it had been given an outer casing of stone, quarried from nearby, and so bore that date over the great iron-studded oak front door. The front garden was rich with flowers and there was a tennis court on which the family and young folk disported themselves.

After Grandfather's death his fellow councillors, invested with temporary power, decided it was the ideal spot to build their new council estate. 'The farm would make a good museum,' suggested one tentatively. It had been mentioned in local history books as being the most interesting building in the area.

'Who ever would want a museum here?' scoffed the others, though now the Blackcountry Museum is one of the most popular in the country. There was then no law for the protection of old buildings and so the farm was demolished, not without dignity, for the great twisted chimneys defied and broke the tackle brought for their destruction.

Having made up my mind I consulted my husband.

* * *

As usual Christmas had caught me napping. Every year I resolved that I would shop in October and write cards in November, leaving me free for the exigencies of December, but I am an improvident creature and never learn by experi-

ence. Hospitals plan a general exodus at this time and discharge patients prematurely, while long-term institutions just let them loose for the festive period. This influx of patients still needing nursing care is one of the burdens of Christmas for the district nurse, and on the day itself essential treatment and care of the very ill must still be carried out.

The day before Christmas Eve I had a call from the nursing supervisor (our Queen Bee) to alert me that the nurse on my adjoining area had gone sick and would I do her relief. It wasn't a question but a command and I was furious. Why me? (Because you were the first one she could cop on the phone, you fool!) As an administrator she was off-duty herself by now and only anxious to pass the buck. In vain I protested, pleading overwork myself, we too had a staff shortage; it all fell on deaf ears. 'You get too involved with your own patients, nurse. You must cut down there,' she answered coldly, putting down the phone.

Troubles never come singly and during the day the car broke down. This was calamitous, in fact outrageous, for it was almost new and I couldn't possibly manage without it. I phoned the garage from whence it had come. Propitiously they agreed to deal with it though warning me that they closed at midday on Christmas Eve, so it must be collected between eleven-thirty and twelve o'clock or I would be without it all over the holiday. Sometimes I thought it would be better not to have a car, for then your limitations were recognized, whereas with a car you were expected to move mountains, and when the wretched vehicle let you down you were still lumbered with the mountain.

The following day, Christmas Eve, I set off very early on foot and hampered with a light raincoat which I could pop over my uniform when I went to fetch the car. I couldn't face Dudley in the conspicuity of my uniform and I certainly wouldn't have time to go home and change, apart from which

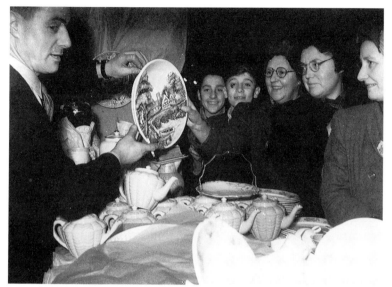

A bargain for the festive season at Dudley Market on Christmas Eve
in 1952

we were not expected to leave our beat while on duty. I
planned to conduct my transformation at Mrs Tibbs; she was
used to my vagaries and accepted them resignedly but not
without curiosity.

'Wheer bin yo gooin?' she demanded as I executed the
quick change, and when I explained, she said:

'Then while yo'm theer get me money back on this.'

Blatantly ignoring my protests she brought forth a cardi-
gan still encased in its cellophane wrapping. She was always
getting her home help to make purchases for her at a certain
store, then a few weeks later she would badger me to return
the dratted things and get her money back. I hate asking for
refunds but it was a service the shop granted without demur
so I usually complied on my day off. But now of all times!

She put the garment into its original bag and thrust it on me. 'I want the money fer me turkey,' she whined, and remembering it would probably be reduced in the after Christmas sale I took it, cursing myself for not having changed elsewhere. I might have known she would turn it to her own advantage. Leaving my hat and nursing bag with her I made for the bus.

En route for the garage I decided to get rid of Mrs Tibbs's parcel first. The store was crowded with Christmas shoppers and as I pushed through the swing doors hot air engulfed me and I was drawn like a helpless swimmer into a whirlpool of humanity. Desperately I surfaced and fought my way to the appropriate counter where a queue waited. When my turn came and I handed over the garment I noticed the price was still on, just over four pounds. The girl after a deft examination of it gave me a chit for five, but when I drew her attention to the discrepancy she rebuked me.

'It's gone up since then, and we always refund the current price. Kindly move on,' and propelled by the basket of the woman behind I moved. That old faggot Mrs Tibbs! However had she cottoned on to this lark of waiting to get her refund when the price would have gone up? One day it would have gone down and then she'd have a shock. I was at the customer service desk in another queue when I realized the time. I ought to have collected the car first, but then I would never have found anywhere to park it. At last I changed my chit for a crisp fiver which I folded and put in my left-hand pocket carefully. I would keep my own money in the right. I was making for the swing doors when I froze. Coming through them was the Queen Bee herself.

'Don't panic,' I told myself sternly. 'Quick! Get behind that clothes rack.' Colourful contraptions concealed me, but what if I was revealed? Shopping when I should be on duty,

especially after prating so about being overworked. I could
have explained the car but not Mrs Tibbs.

'You must not get so involved with your own patients,
nurse.' How right she was and she was coming nearer. I
snatched a bright pink satin blouse off the rack and held it up
before my face as though inspecting it; later when peering
cautiously round it I saw her proceeding upstairs to the lin-
gerie. I made a dash for the doors, impeded all the way, and
then I had some difficulty getting through. With a sense of
guilt I realized that in my haste I had pushed aside a heavily
pregnant girl and with apologies I stepped back and held the
door ajar for her. It was then I saw what had hindered my
progress. I was still holding the pink satin blouse! As I stared
at it in horror a hand gripped my shoulder and I shrank from
the condemning countenance of what was obviously the store
detective.

No! Never! This couldn't happen to me!

I felt sick and faint and unable to defend myself. The shop
whirled and my knees had no substance.

'I didn't do it!' I bleated nauseously but the detective's lip
curled and a crowd gathered sensing a kill (and where was the
Queen Bee now?). I visualized the headlines: 'Nurse caught
shoplifting.' Gun-layer would never forgive me – and what
about my family?

'Please God get me out of this! I will be good. You know I
never pinch anything – well, perhaps a bit of white lint here
and there – and that baby cream from the clinic to rub on my
hands – everybody does – I'll take it back, I promise – *Please*
God!'

The pregnant girl had come forward and challenged my
captor.

'Yo' cor charge 'er, 'ers inside the doors.'

'She wasn't, and still has one foot outside.'

'Yo've got t'ave both outside.'

The pregnant one obviously knew her rights. She turned to me. 'I'll come ter court with yer.' Court! Good heavens!

The crowds were joining in with seasonal good humour. 'Goo on, give the wench a break! It's Christmas.' Jocularly they bunted the detective. 'Strewth! 'ers started!'

My pregnant friend had suddenly bent two-double, clutching her belly and emitting an agonized 'Moo.'

For the first time the store detective's face took on a human expression: it registered horror.

'Get out! Both of you!' and snatching the blouse from me, 'I must admit I never knew anyone take one on a hanger before!'

Outside on the pavement, still supporting the girl, I became articulate again, pouring out my relief and gratitude, but she would have none of it.

'Gotta stick together, aye we? she grinned. She was making a remarkable recovery but the least I could do was offer her a lift home. I explained about the car and the urgent need to collect it.

'Then I'll wait for yer,' she said. 'Over theer, by the WC,' and she indicated the public convenience over the road. I rushed off gutterwise to avoid the crowded pavements and only just made it. The garage was about to close for Christmas but the car was waiting and roadworthy once more. Behind the wheel I felt secure again, as though I had awakened from a nightmare, and in a long cavalcade of traffic, bumper to bumper, I made slow progress back through the town, light-headed and buoyant with relief.

'What about me?' nudged God at my elbow.

'Bless you, God, and thank you. I won't forget.'

When I drew alongside the loo my friend was just coming up the steps. She was as flat as a pancake and carrying two bulging shopping bags which had been empty before. Blithely ignoring the toots of irate drivers she nipped across

the road and slumped thankfully into the seat beside me. The tent-like coat hung open now, revealing a long knitted tubular garment which hung flatly about her lean body like a deflated balloon. The shopping bags which she'd plonked between her legs disclosed a multitude of unwrapped very new garments.

'Whatever will you do with all those?' I gasped, easing back into the traffic.

'Why get the money back on 'em at the West Bromwich an' Brummagem stores!' she laughed.

'Now if I were you', I advised knowledgeably, 'I should hang on to them for a bit. They're sure to go up in price before long.'

Mrs Tibbs was delighted with the five pound notes I gave her.

The crisp fiver had disappeared into thin air.

Christmas Eve

ALICE LUNT

This extract comes from Secret Stepmother, *a story written for girls, many of whom Alice Lunt was teaching English at Oldbury County Secondary School when this book was first published in 1959. Author of many children's stories, Alice Lunt originally came from Lancashire until moving to the Midlands to do her teacher training at Worcester.*

'Time to get up,' sighed Beth Lloyd.

She lay there for a moment, planning her day. There were mince-pies to be made, and parsley and breadcrumbs to be prepared for tomorrow's turkey. She must whisk round with a duster. There was last-minute shopping. But Janet would keep the younger children from under her feet, and Simon would be back in time to help with the Christmas parcels.

There was a gentle *tap-tap* on her door. She raised her head from the pillow and called, 'Come in!'

'Cup of tea,' said Janet.

'Good gracious, girl! Up already?'

'We've been up for ages. We've lit the fire. Cathie's cooking breakfast and I'm going to dress the boys.' Janet sat on the edge of the bed, grinning triumphantly.

'You're supposed to be on holiday. You'll have to be up terribly early when you start work in the Nursery.'

'I might as well get used to it. Think of all the years in hospital when I'm a real nurse. That's if I ever get through the exams.'

'Oh, you'll get through. After all, you can put in a good deal of studying before you're eighteen. And you won't be the only one. Hazel will have to work just as hard.'

Janet laughed. 'I suppose you know that you'll have to spend half your time helping us.'

'All right, all right!' said Beth. 'I'm not complaining.'

'I can hear the boys. I'd better go. By the way, do you want any help with the baking?'

'If you'll keep the boys out of the kitchen, I can make *nine hundred* mince-pies. Rolling pastry is their latest craze, and I just can't cope with them today. I thought I'd do the baking this morning and go to the shops this afternoon.'

'I'll look after the boys if you'll promise not to come into the living-room without warning.'

Beth laughed. 'Whatever are you up to?'

'Secrets,' said Janet.

Her stepmother knew the nature of the 'secrets'. The children had been preparing for Christmas for several days. Small purchases had been hidden away in the girls' chest of drawers and Janet had laid in a supply of coloured paper and string. Even Harry, who always saved his pocket-money, had raided his money-box so that he could buy presents for the family. Beth knew that he had kept two or three shillings in reserve, and this worried her a little, for the other children were willing to give away their last halfpennies at Christmas-time. Then she told herself not to be silly, for already Harry had improved beyond their wildest dreams. A short while ago it seemed that only Janet existed for him. Now they all had a share in his affections and sometimes Johnnie and he played together without quarrelling.

Oldbury's Birmingham Street following a snowfall in about 1910

When she went downstairs on that morning of 24th December, Beth Lloyd was pleased at the way Christmas had begun. In the kitchen another surprise awaited her. The potatoes were peeled, the carrots scraped. Everything had been left beautifully tidy. In the living-room Cathie was putting the cosy on the teapot, and a dish of bacon and tomatoes was keeping warm on the hearth.

'This is wonderful!' she cried. 'A sort of advance Christmas present.'

Cathie beamed at her. 'Has Janet told you what we're going to do after breakfast? It's a good job Dad isn't back yet. I don't know where we'd put him. We'll *try* to get finished before he arrives, but there's ever such a lot to do.'

Indeed the four of them were occupied with their own mysterious affairs the whole morning. At lunch-time the living-room was littered with scraps of paper and string.

kmk

'Maybe I'd better. The shops will be getting more and more crowded.'

'I'm going shopping,' announced Harry.

Beth's eyes widened in alarm. Once Harry got an idea into his head . . . ! 'No, dear,' she said. 'I'll take you with me another day. There are too many people in the shops this afternoon, and I'm in a dreadful hurry.'

He shook his head and stated politely but firmly: 'I'm going with you today.'

'Not today, dear.'

'Yes,' said Harry.

'But why, dear?'

'I've got to do my shopping.'

'What do you want to buy?'

'It's a secret.'

'All right, I'll take him,' said Janet. 'I don't suppose we'll be more than a few minutes.'

Again Harry shook his head. 'I've to go with Mother. It's very important.'

Beth and Janet looked at each other helplessly.

'Do you know what all this is about, Cathie?' asked Beth, turning to her.

Cathie grinned. 'I've no idea.'

In the end it was curiosity, as much as anything else, that made Beth give way to him. He trotted contentedly at her side, one hand in hers, the other hand clutching the money in his coat pocket. To her surprise he made no attempt to interfere with her plans, but waited patiently at shop counters until the harassed assistants had dealt with her.

When they had pushed their way out of the sweet-shop she said: 'Now I've spent all my money. What about you?'

'Come with me,' said Harry, tugging her towards the door of a small shop.

'But, laddie, that's a jeweller's!'

'I've got to go here,' he persisted.

Releasing her hand, he dived into the shop. Beth gasped, took a firm grip on her basket, and followed him. He was standing on tiptoe, so that his chin was on a level with the counter. The shop assistant, a kindly looking, middle-aged woman, was leaning over to him.

Beth heard his whisper. 'I want to buy my mother a ring.'

The assistant answered him in whispers. 'Is that your mother?' She nodded towards Beth. 'What kind of a ring did you want for her?'

'A diamond ring.'

'How much money have you got?'

'Two and threepence halfpenny.'

The woman looked grave. 'I'm afraid we haven't any diamond rings at that price, but I'll tell you what we have got. We've a very old, valuable ring in a sort of silver. I'll show it to you.' Harry peeped at Beth, who pretended to be absorbed

in a tray of second-hand brooches. 'There!' said the assistant, showing him an attractive little ring in dull metal. 'It's supposed to be lucky,' she whispered.

'How much is it?'

'Two and threepence halfpenny. Would you like her to try it on?'

Harry beckoned wildly. Beth came towards him, praying that the ring was the correct size.

'Whatever are you doing, Harry?'

'I'm buying you a ring,' he said.

'Not this one? But how lovely!' She let him slip it on to the third finger of her right hand. 'Why, it's a perfect fit!'

'Would you like me to put it in a box?' asked the assistant.

'Oh, no,' said Harry. 'She'll want to wear it.'

Two very tired people climbed the stairs. Everything was ready for Christmas Day, but they wanted to have a last look at their sleeping children. There was nothing to be seen but dark heads on white pillows, and dark, bulging shapes hanging over the foot of the beds. There was no sound but that of quiet breathing.

In the second room, with Simon's arm about her waist, Beth looked down at the little boys. She touched first her wedding-ring, then the new ring on her right hand.

'Simon,' she murmured.

'Yes, darling?'

'I like our children,' she said.

Winter

WILLIAM SHENSTONE

*Landscape gardening, letter writing and poetry were the great
pursuits of the Halesowen contemporary of Dr Samuel Johnson.
The Lichfield literary giant taught in nearby Stourbridge,
attended the same Oxford college as Shenstone, and later
produced a brief memoir of his fellow writer.*

No more, ye warbling birds! rejoice:
Of all that cheer'd the plain,
Echo alone preserves her voice,
And she – repeats my pain.

Where'er my lovesick limbs I lay
To shun the rushing wind,
Its busy murmurs seem to say,
'She never will be kind!'

The Naiads, o'er their frozen urns,
In icy chains repine;
And each in sullen silence mourns
Her freedom lost, like mine!

Soon will the sun's returning rays
The cheerless frost control;
When will relenting Delia chase
The winter of my soul?

47

Warley Woods, three miles north west of The Leasowes, were
likewise landscaped thirty years after Shenstone's death, by architect
Humphrey Repton

Christmas Mumming Play

FREDERICK W. HACKWOOD

Another lengthier extract about Christmas comes from Frederick Hackwood who describes a typical Black Country mumming play. This particular version was performed recently as part of Christmas festivities in Smethwick.

As in the later centuries it has been customary for the theatre to abandon the legitimate drama at Christmas time in favour of pantomime, so in olden days it was the practice of the Mummers to present a special Christmas Play suitable for indoor presentation - in both cases the characters being drawn from legend and romance, and the plot being generally a medley of more or less incoherent episodes loosely strung together.

In the north of the county the Mummers were usually known as Guisers. The nineteenth century Mummers in these Folk Plays went round from house to house, asking permission to play their Mumming in kitchens of private houses, or in some large room of a public-house. They were dressed fantastically in paper and tinsel, and coloured rags; some with blacked and some with floured faces; some wearing masks; some with false beards and wigs. The combat was done with broad-bladed wooden swords, with the flat of which a good sounding whack could be given.

In the older days of 'Merrie England' the commodious halls
of the squirearchy afforded a more convenient stage for the
presentation of these old mumming plays. And they were
always popular, as the old ballad informs us:

> To shorten winter's sadness,
> See where the folks with gladness,
> Disguised all are coming
> Right wantonly a-mumming –
> Fa lal la!

One of these Christmas Mumming Plays, last seen performed
in the bar parlour of a Wednesbury tavern in 1879, was but little
removed from the common type, in title, or plot, or dialogue.
Here is the Black Country version of the old theme:

GOOD ST GEORGE AND THE BOLD HECTOR

Enter (after a loud knock at the door).
Open-the-Door.

O-t-Door:
The first that doth step in is good old
   Open-the-door,
And, lads, if you'll believe me well, I've
   opened many a score.

(With sly wink and gesture at this.
He next proceeds to clear an open space
for the other actors, who have now
followed him in, but leave him the centre
of the stage.)

Give room, give room, in this gallant
   hall, give us room to play,

And you shall see a right Merry Masque
   Upon this happy Christmas Day.
So shift the chairs, and make a good
   wide ring.
That you may see us well, both act, and
   dance, and sing.
Silence, brave gents and lovely ladies
   fair! Now give an eye,
To see and hear our queer, quaint
   comico – tragedie.

(He retires. St George takes centre of stage.)

St George:
Here come I, St George approved of old,
A Knight of valour and virtue, stout and
   bold.
Many the gallant deeds that I have done,
Clean victories, both east and west, that
   I have won.
In deadly marsh, and eke on sandy plain,
Giants, griffins and rocs in swarms I've
   slain –
'Twas I that brought the famed dreaded
   dragon to slaughter,
For which I gained the Egyptian
   Monarch's handsome daughter.

(Enter to him Bold Hector.)

Hector:
Who's this that boasts in Hector's
   hearing?
Of all braves and braggarts, I'll soon
   make a clearing!

I am bold Hector! Bold Hector is my
name,
And with my trusty sword, I always win
the game!

(Enter, smartly Slasher.)

Slasher:
The game, Sir? What game, Sir? This
game's not in your power,
The brave St George will slash and slay
you dead within the hour!

(Enter, stately, the Black Prince.)

Prince:
Not so fast, my gallant lads and heroes
all!
Fair's fair, brave's brave; but when you
try a fall,
Sides and chances equal, for Englishmen
is reckoned –
So to see all things square, I'll act for one
as Second.

Slasher:
Well said, most noble prince. To make
the combat square,
You second good St George, and I will
see Bold Hector fair.

*(The two Principals and two Seconds
prepare their arms.)*
(Enter, deliberately, Safety Sam.)

A Black Country Christmas

Sam:

Hear one last word for peace from Safety
   Sam of Staffordshire!
Peace is a noble thing, though it may be
   bought too dear.
So ere to mortal strife, these noble
   gallants do repair,
'May God defend the right!' be our one
   and only prayer.

(Enter, with roguish sidling shuffle, Beelzebub.)

Beelzebub:

Here comes I, sly old Beelzebub!
Over my shoulder I carries my club,
And in my hand a frying pan –
So don't you think I'm a jolly old man?
If you think I'm cutting it rather fat,
Just drop a penny in the old man's hat –
A useful penny it is you'll then lay out,
If you want to see the whole of our fine
   play out.

*(Enter, impishly and perkily, the little
Blue Dwarf.)*

Dwarf:

Stand off, stand off! I've fought ten
   thousand duels on The Delves,
And all you knaves that want to fight,
   had best defend yourselves.
No foe stands up but I'll smash and hash
   him as small as flies,
And sell his vile carcase to make into
   nice mince pies –

Mince pies hot, mince pies cold,
Good mince pies at ten days old!

(Black Prince coolly lifts him up bodily,
throws him into the arms of Beelzebub,
who carries him out. The two champions,
St George and Bold Hector, and
their seconds, Black Prince and Slasher,
take the centre, and the combat begins.
The fencing is done with much dancing
round the ring, loud clashing of swords,
and the excited shouts of the other
actors. After many fierce lunges and
rapid parries, and cracks on the head
and legs with the flat of the swords,
Hector is stabbed and falls prone.)

Slasher:
O champion saint, O holy George! what
    hast thou done?
Thou hast gone and slain my dear, my
    only son!
He was indeed my first-born, and my
    true-begotten heir –
I cannot, will not, idly stand and see
    him bleeding there!
A doctor, a doctor! I'll give ten
    thousand pound,
If but a good and learned doctor can be
    found!

(Enter, slowly and sedately, the Doctor.)

Doctor:
Here come I, the great and learned
    Doctor Brown,

The cleverest, safest doctor in all the
    town.
Crutches for lame ducks make I, and
    spectacles for poor blind bats,
Also barber-leech I am, to shave and
    bleed all pussy cats.
I've travelled far, in Italy, Titaly,
    Dudley Port, and Old Spain,
But right glad I am to be once more in
    Old Wednesbury again.

Slasher:
What diseases, sir, are they you cure?

Doctor:
Why, all diseases known, you may be
    sure:
The gout, the scurvy, and the ptysic,
And all of them without a drop of physic.
So [taking Hector gravely and skilfully
    by the hand] you get up, sir, and sing
    that fine old song,
Of one who's not been dead for very
    long.

Hector (*rising erect again*):
Once was I dead, but now I am alive,
God bless the Doctor, who made me to
    survive!
Through his great art, I was not dead for
    very long,
And so to prove his skill, let me sing to
    you a live man's song!

(*Sings some popular song of the day, which
has a chorus in which all can join.*)

Beelzebub:

Our play is played, and now we've done,
We hope we've given you lots of simple
  fun.
So if you think at all it's really funny,
You'll fill our empty pokes with lots of
  money.
Send us away, please, now that all is
  calm,
And sly old Beelzebub 'll do you no
  harm.
Take notice that we've got no leathern
  bottle,
And nothing was poured down the dead
  man's throttle.
For your fun 'twas he fought, and got
  himself slain,
For your money he'll rise and fight his
  battles o'er again.
We hope this nonsense your spirits will
  joyful rouse,
So we bid you Good-day, and Peace be
  on this noble house!

*(All join hands to dance round, to the
accompaniment of some other popular
song – which at the end is changed to
one to which they march out, Beelzebub
collecting the largesse in his frying pan.)*

In the *Folk Lore Journal*, Vol. IV, p. 350, is printed a
Christmas Guiser's Play of the same date emanating from
Eccleshall, and which is virtually the same dramatic story,
though not quite as good in plot or dialogue. In the northern
version the characters are called Open-door, Old Beelzebub,

Little Doctor, King George, Noble Soldier, Black Prince of Paradise, Little Jack Devil-doubt, and Sing Ghiles (? Sir Guy of Warwick). As usual, the action includes much challenging to fight and clashing of swords. The finale in this case is a chorus (the music is given), 'On a bleak and a cold frosty morning'.

The main object of these performances was always to collect largesse, and the performers therefore sought popularity by 'playing to the gallery', as the professional actors express it.

Letters Home

HAROLD PARRY

There seems some extra poignancy about the short-lived careers of the First World War poets. The Bloxwich soldier Harold Parry seemed destined for literary fame after a brilliant academic career at Queen Mary's Grammar School, Walsall, and Oxford University but he was killed barely five months after these letters home.

17th K.R.R., B.E.F., France,
9th December, 1916.

MY DEAREST MOTHER,
I got your letter together with one from father, yesterday, and I was rather glad, as I had not heard from anyone for four days. You also say that you haven't heard from me since the

25th, wherefore there must be several letters, or rather notes, on the way which in all probability you will have already received before you get this.

The weather here has been somewhat depressing of late, and I have been wet through three days in succession on parade. We have had a series of inspections by various big bugs – most deplorably boring efforts – and it has always rained while we have been standing and waiting for the aforesaid Generals (and staff – one must never forget the staff) to arrive.

It is the privilege of Generals to arrive late, although punctuality, I believe, is one of the standard military dictums of etiquette. However, it's all in the game, and so we don't mind over much, though it will of certainty be more than merely nice to feel oneself a free man again after the war is ended.

News of late is fascinating, though perhaps a trifle unpalatable; but there are things going on behind the scenes of which we wot not, and just now Horatio Bottomley is in favour with the men because of his prognostications of peace within ten weeks. It would of a certainty be most interesting to know what all these changes in Allied diplomatic circles mean and whither they are tending.

In the meantime, while we speculate perhaps a little idly, France gets muddier and muddier, and the ceaseless thunder of the guns orchestrates noisily (with variation and exceptions) along the whole of the vast battle fronts of Europe, and everyone – Germany not excepted – waits, Micawber-like, for something to turn up – something which will end the war.

As for myself, though leave seems impossible now until well into the new year, I can manage to carry on until the time and season in which I shall be able to see all dear things again, and for a brief period be able to lounge in the old flannel bags and old blazer. However much you may think it time I appeared in the glory of a new turnout, I'm quite sure you

will understand my desire to turn out in the same delectable, though perhaps a trifle worn, garments of the old days. They are inevitably associated with better days, and in my mind I dwell upon the day when I shall don them again with an altogether inordinate longing.

I'm very sorry to hear, mother mine, that you are not well; but however much you feel the twinges of rheumatism, if it gives you any comfort, you know full well that I always look forward to your letters and love you for them. It must take a big effort when you're not feeling well to sit down and write a long and cheery letter to me, and I appreciate the letter the more for it.

But keep cheerful, mother – have a good time this Christmas, and think that the star of Bethlehem still shines, and the God that gave His dear and only Son to the world does not look upon this war unmoved and from afar. This war is none of God's making – it is of the people's; and God, this day and all days, is down on earth amongst us, suffering our anguish and joying in our joy. The arm that has protected me thus far is still as potent to protect; wherefore, even in the most miserable of times, I can be happy and can contrive to live in a joyful past and a no less joyous future.

I must close now – I've tons of work to do. Give my love to all at home and to all my friends.

Your affectionate son,
HAL.

17th K.R.R., B.E.F., FRANCE,
1st January, 1917.

MY DEAREST MOTHER,

I haven't been able to write for three or four days, becos' we've been in the line again, but now I'm away back quite near the place where we had our three weeks' rest. I've been detailed to attend a general course here, and I may be out of the line for a

month with any luck. I've an excellent billet, a beautiful bed, and most amiable people in the house, with whom I get on very well. My French is improving rapidly with talking to the owners of the house, who lost one son early on in the war.

I spent a rotten Christmas night. There was a big artillery 'strafe' by the Bosche all along our front, and we had a somewhat lively and uncomfortable time, but for the next three days we had a very quiet time.

My address whilst here will still be the same, and letters and parcels will be forwarded to me from the battalion.

I had an extraordinary journey down here – a journey well worth description. I left the trenches just as dusk was falling and the first Verey lights were going up along the line. After walking along a muddy road for about a mile we picked up a Maltese cart, which we promptly boarded, since it was going in our direction. It was a lovely night, quite warm, and the crescent moon shone between the flocks of fleecy clouds which hurried and scurried across the sky. The two horses – the first of which, being 'leader', was mounted – jogged steadily along, and the countryside passed by in panorama. I got the curious feeling that it was not we who were moving, but the landscape. We passed through a deserted and battered village; the moon shone quietly between the broken walls and battered roofs and made the whole scene one of acute desolation. The solitary soldier on traffic duty at the cross-roads only served to enliven his immediate neighbourhood and the rest of the village seemed more forlorn by contrast. We clattered out of the village and after a time came upon scattered farms which were inhabited. Then we splashed our way through a stream which had overflowed its banks and had flooded the road. Here we paused for a while to help some people, less fortunate than ourselves, who had missed the road and become fast stuck in the mud of the wayside.

Eventually we arrived at a big town, about two miles from our transport lines, where we were to spend the night. We got

A Black Country Christmas

FOURTH ANNUAL CHRISTMAS

Dinner & Concert

Under the patronage of

The Mayor and Mayoress of Walsall (Coun. and Mrs. A. J. Llewellen),
Sir Richard A. Cooper, Bart., M.P., Lady Cooper, Col. R. S. Williamson, V.D.,
Lieut.-Col. H. E. Twentyman, C.O., Capt. and Adjt. S. J. Hattin,
Lieut. Qr.-M. E. W. Kirby, Capt. H. Ashmole Ashmall,
Capt. S. E. Loxton, A.S.C., M.T. (V.), Lieut. T. B. Buxton, Lieut. H. P. Hooper,
2nd Lieut. A. C. Fraser Wood, 2nd Lieut. R. B. Sutton,
2nd Lieut. H. R. Aulton, 2nd Lieut. C. L. Hodgkinson, and the
N.C.O's. and Members of "A" Company 1st Vol. Batt. South Staffs. Regt.

IN THE

TEMPERANCE HALL, WALSALL

ON

Saturday, December 28th, 1918

FOR THE

DISABLED SAILORS AND SOLDIERS.

Dinner at 5 p.m.   Concert at 6-30 p.m.

Committee :

C. Sergt.-Major W. Ashwell (Chairman), R. Sergt.-Major W. A. Lancaster,
R. Q.-M. Sergt. C. Heap, R. Q.-M. Sergt. D. W. McAlister,
C.S.M.I.M. F. Foster, C. Q.-M. Sergt. F. Busst, Sergts. S. Aston, W. Gretton,
F. Y. Wood, J. H. Freeman, H. A. Vipond, W. Preston, P. A. Marshall,
H. N. Grove, Corpls. S. C. Sergeant, J. M. Laker, E. E. Skett,
L.-Corpl T. H. Porter, Privates Jeff C. Crooke, W. H. Thacker, J. S. Bird,
A. G. Smith and W. H. Haughton.

Hon. Secretary	–	Leonard I. Aulton, 95, Wednesbury Road, Walsall.
M.C.	–	R. Sergt.-Major W. A. Lancaster.

T. Richmond, Walsall.

Dinner and concert programme, 1918

61

out and made our way to a restaurant, where, for a matter of five francs, we had an excellent dinner. After dinner we walked to the transport lines, and though already many miles behind the line we could see the Verey lights going up along the whole front. It was a remarkable sight, one to be seen to be appreciated.

Next morning after a good sleep – on the floor-boards of a tent – and a better breakfast we got into an already crowded motor lorry, and, pitching and rocking, we thumped our way along for four hours until at last, in the midst of a most wonderful sunset – a sunset which covered the land with gold and purple and red – we arrived at our destination, and now – *me voilà!* – out of the line, living a somewhat more civilised and very much more cleanly life again. The course may last for a month. I hope it will, since it promises to be both interesting and comfortable, two virtues much beprized of soldiers. And so I will sit in this comfortable old farmhouse, exchanging occasional words with the old farmer, and writing to you people at home, people who are never out of my thoughts and whom I am waiting to meet and see and speak with again. However comfortable one may be out here, one is still an exile, and however nice the inhabitants are to us they can never fill one tithe of the vacant spaces in our lives, spaces which the loved ones at home have made for themselves, and which none others can fill or hope to fill. I must stop now. I haven't much time before dinner, but I will write again as soon as possible. For the present I commend you all to the care of One who has me in His care.

Your affectionate son,
HAL.

Also in the memorial volume of Parry's verses and letters comes this almost prophetic poem which seems, in the words of that book's foreword, 'to honour, in the sad permanence of print, his way of living and his manner of death'.

THE NORTH WIND

When Winter drags her chariot wheel
Through the deep snow,
And skies are blue as hard, cold steel,
And North Winds blow,
Keep faith – some day the world will mend
Your broken mind;
Keep faith – for maybe grief will end
With the North Wind.

An Old-World Grandfather

SIR HENRY NEWBOLT

The Bilston-born poet, official naval historian, novelist and lawyer, Sir Henry Newbolt, is best remembered in the popular imagination for his Drake's Drum. *His father, the local vicar, died when the future poet was only four. The young Henry then went to live in Walsall at his grandparents' house – 'not a large one, but it had the quiet dignity to match those who lived in it'. His grandfather's sense of dignity at Christmas time is described here in an extract from Sir Henry's memoirs.*

Lastly there comes clearly to my mind the parlour, the scene of parlour tea, when we drank – even the youngest and most

dangerous of us – out of superb old Derby china, and were each given a whole round of the loaf spread thick with jam. 'You will make them ill', my mother used to say, and grandmamma's invariable answer was that good jam was a wholesome as good butter – an opinion also expressed publicly by Mr Gladstone, but twenty years later. In this same room, I remember being present at a Christmas dinner, at which my grandfather not only presided but carved – as I afterwards saw Lord Grimthorpe do, so late as 1889 – carved every dish with his own hand. With sixteen at table and many dishes, this took some time, and the more because my grandfather kept faithfully to the old provincial etiquette. As each portion was carried to the guest for whom it was carved, the courteous voice followed it from the head of the table – 'Cousin Partridge, have I sent you what you like?' And the formula came in reply, 'Thank you, Sir, an excellent cut.' 'Cousin Partridge' was 'a poor relation' and sat at the bottom of the line, but he was treated with all the honours – 'A glass of wine with you, Cousin' – in acknowledgement, as I now suspect, that although he had foolishly taken orders and had but 'a poor living', he too came of one of the old civic families and bore a name that could be found upon the list of Mayors, a century back.

At the time, not a glimmer of this suspicion reached my mind – I was only six years old, and though my feelings and instincts were alert, my observation of motives and characters was decidedly superficial. All that I heard spoken I took at its face value – I had had no experience of insincerity or even of 'shrewd comment'. On the day of which I have been speaking, my mother presented me after dinner to 'my Cousin Partridge' and started a pleasant conversation between us: she afterwards told me she was glad I had liked him, and that he was the best man in the room, whatever the rest might think of him.

Second Thoughts of an Idle Fellow

JEROME K. JEROME

Walsall's great humorist, Jerome K. Jerome, here presents a largely tongue-in-cheek suggestion by one of his characters for the abolition of Christmas. The Idle Thoughts of an Idle Fellow *was published in 1889, nine years before these 'second' offerings. Although honoured in his lifetime with the freedom of his native borough, the famous novelist did live in another Black Country town, Stourbridge, before his eventual move to the metropolis.*

'Did I walk into you?' he asked surprised.

'Well, not right in,' I answered, 'if we are to be literal. You walked on to me; if I had not stopped you, I suppose you would have walked over me.'

'It is this confounded Christmas business,' he explained. 'It drives me off my head.'

'I have heard Christmas advanced as an excuse for many things,' I replied, 'but not early in September.'

'Oh, you know what I mean,' he answered, 'we are in the middle of our Christmas number. I am working day and night upon it. By the bye,' he added, 'that puts me in mind. I am

65

arranging a symposium, and I want you to join. "Should Christmas,"' – I interrupted him.

'My dear fellow,' I said, 'I commenced my journalistic career when I was eighteen, and I have continued it at intervals ever since. I have written about Christmas from the sentimental point of view; I have analyzed it from the philosophical point of view; and I have scarified it from the sarcastic standpoint. I have treated Christmas humorously for the Comics, and sympathetically for the Provincial Weeklies. I have said all that is worth saying on the subject of Christmas – maybe a trifle more. I have told the new-fashioned Christmas story – you know the sort of thing: your heroine tries to understand herself, and, failing, runs off with the man who began as the hero; your good woman turns out to be really bad when one comes to know her; while the villain, the only decent person in the story, dies with an enigmatic sentence on his lips that looks as if it meant something, but which you yourself would be sorry to have to explain. I have also written the old-fashioned Christmas story – you know that also; you begin with a good old-fashioned snowstorm; you have a good old-fashioned squire, and he lives in a good old-fashioned Hall; you work in a good old-fashioned murder; and end up with a good old-fashioned Christmas dinner. I have gathered Christmas guests together round the crackling logs to tell ghost stories to each other on Christmas Eve, while without the wind howled, as it always does on these occasions, at its proper cue. I have sent children to Heaven on Christmas Eve – it must be quite a busy time for St Peter, Christmas morning, so many good children die on Christmas Eve. It has always been a popular night with them. – I have revivified dead lovers and brought them back well and jolly, just in time to sit down to the Christmas dinner. I am not ashamed of having done these things. At the time I thought them good. I once loved currant wine and girls with tousley

hair. One's views change as one grows older. I have discussed Christmas as a religious festival. I have arranged it as a social incubus. If there by any joke connected with Christmas that I have not already made I should be glad to hear it. I have trotted out the indigestion jokes till the sight of one of them gives me indigestion myself. I have ridiculed the family gathering. I have scoffed at the Christmas present. I have made witty use of paterfamilias and his bills. I have –'

'Did I ever show you,' I broke off to ask as we were crossing the Haymarket, 'that little parody of mine on Poe's poem of 'The Bells'? It begins –' He interrupted me in his turn –

'Bills, bills, bills,' he repeated.

'You are quite right,' I admitted. 'I forgot I ever showed it to you.'

'You never did,' he replied.

'Then how do you know how it begins?' I asked.

'I don't know for certain,' he admitted, 'but I get, on an average, sixty-five a year submitted to me, and they all begin that way. I thought, perhaps, yours did also.'

'I don't see how else it could begin,' I retorted. He had rather annoyed me. 'Besides, it doesn't matter how a poem begins. It is how it goes on that is the important thing; and anyhow, I'm not going to write you anything about Christmas. Ask me to make you a new joke about a plumber; suggest my inventing something original and not too shocking for a child to say about heaven; propose my running you off a dog story that can be believed by a man of average determination, and we may come to terms. But on the subject of Christmas I am taking a rest.'

By this time we had reached Piccadilly Circus.

'I don't blame you,' he said, 'if you are as sick of the subject as I am. So soon as these Christmas numbers are off my mind, and Christmas is over till next June at the office, I shall begin it at home. The housekeeping is gone up a pound a week

An early 1900s view of Dudley's Priory Road

already. I know what that means. The dear little woman is saving up to give me an expensive present that I don't want. I think the presents are the worst part of Christmas. Emma will give me a water-colour that she has painted herself. She always does. There would be no harm in that if she did not expect me to hang it in the drawing room. Have you ever seen my cousin Emma's water-colours?' he asked.

'I think I have,' I replied.

'There's no thinking about it,' he retorted angrily. 'They're not the sort of water-colours you forget.'

He apostrophized the Circus generally.

'Why do people do these things?' he demanded. 'Even an amateur artist must have *some* sense. Can't they see what is happening? There's that thing of hers hanging in the passage. I put it in the passage because there's not much light in the

passage. She's labelled it Reverie. If she had called it Influenza I could have understood it. I asked her where she got the idea from, and she said she saw the sky like that one evening in Norfolk. Great Heavens! then why didn't she shut her eyes, or go home and hide behind the bed-curtains? If I had seen a sky like that in Norfolk I should have taken the first train back to London. I suppose the poor girl can't help seeing these things, but why paint them?'

I said, 'I suppose painting is a necessity to some natures.'

'But why give the things to me?' he pleaded.

I could offer him no adequate reason.

'The idiotic presents that people give you!' he continued. 'I said I'd like Tennyson's poems one year. They had worried me to know what I did want. I didn't want anything really; that was the only thing I could think of that I wasn't dead sure I didn't want. Well, they clubbed together, four of them, and gave me Tennyson in twelve volumes, illustrated with coloured photographs. They meant kindly, of course. If you suggest a tobacco-pouch they give you a blue velvet bag capable of holding about a pound, embroidered with flowers, life-size. The only way one could use it would be to put a strap to it and wear it as a satchel. Would you believe it, I have got a velvet smoking-jacket, ornamented with forget-me-nots and butterflies in coloured silk; I'm not joking. And they ask me why I never wear it. I'll bring it down to the Club one of these nights and wake the place up a bit: it needs it.'

We had arrived by this at the steps of the 'Devonshire'.

'And I'm just as bad', he went on, 'when I give presents. I never give them what they want. I never hit upon anything that is of any use to anybody. If I give Jane a chinchilla tippet, you may be certain chinchilla is the most out-of-date fur that any woman could wear. "Oh! that is nice of you," she says; "now that is just the very thing I wanted. I will keep it by me till chinchilla comes in again." I give the girls watch-chains

when nobody is wearing watch-chains. When watch-chains are all the rage I give them ear-rings, and they thank me, and suggest my taking them to a fancy-dress ball, that being their only chance to wear the confounded things. I waste money on white gloves with black backs, to find that white gloves with black backs stamp a woman as suburban. I believe all the shop-keepers in London save their old stock to palm it off on me at Christmas time. And why does it always take half-a-dozen people to serve you with a pair of gloves, I'd like to know? Only last week Jane asked me to get her some gloves for that last Mansion House affair. I was feeling amiable, and I thought I would do the thing handsomely. I hate going into a draper's shop; everybody stares at a man as if he were forcing his way into the ladies' department of a Turkish bath. One of those marionette sort of men came up to me and said it was a fine morning. What the devil did I want to talk about the morning to him for? I said I wanted some gloves. I described them to the best of my recollection. I said, "I want them four buttons, but they are not to be button-gloves; the buttons are in the middle and they reach up to the elbow, if you know what I mean." He bowed, and said he understood exactly what I meant, which was a damned sight more than I did. I told him I wanted three pair cream and three pair fawn-coloured, and the fawn-coloured were to be swedes. He corrected me. He said I meant "Suede". I dare say he was right, but the interruption put me off, and I had to begin over again. He listened attentively until I had finished. I guess I was about five minutes standing with him there close to the door. He said, "Is that all you require, sir, this morning?" I said it was.

"Thank you, sir," he replied. "This way, please, sir."

'He took me into another room, and there we met a man named Jansen, to whom he briefly introduced me as a gentleman who "desired gloves". "Yes, sir," said Mr Jansen; "and what sort of gloves do you desire?"

An early twentieth-century snowscene at Caldmore Green in Walsall

I told him I wanted six pairs altogether – three suede, fawn-coloured, and three cream-coloured – kids.

He said, "Do you mean kid gloves, sir, or gloves for children?"

He made me angry by that. I told him I was not in the habit of using slang. Nor am I when buying gloves. He said he was sorry. I explained to him about the buttons, so far as I could understand it myself, and about the length. I asked him to see to it that the buttons were sewn on firmly, and that the stitching everywhere was perfect, adding that the last gloves my wife had had of his firm had been most unsatisfactory. Jane had impressed upon me to add that. She said it would make them more careful.

He listened to me in rapt ecstacy. I might have been music.

"And what size, sir?" he asked.

I had forgotten that. "Oh, sixes," I answered, "unless they are very stretchy indeed, in which case they had better be five and three-quarter."

"Oh, and the stitching on the cream is to be black," I added. That was another thing I had forgotten.

"Thank you very much," said Mr Jansen; "is there anything else that you require this morning?"

"No, thank you," I replied, "not this morning." I was beginning to like the man.

He took me for quite a walk, and wherever we went everybody left off what they were doing to stare at me. I was getting tired when we reached the glove department. He marched me up to a young man who was sticking pins into himself. He said "Gloves," and disappeared through a curtain. The young man left off sticking pins into himself, and leant across the counter.

"Ladies' gloves or gentlemen's gloves?" he said.

Well, I was pretty mad by this time, as you can guess. It is funny when you come to think of it afterwards, but the wonder then was that I didn't punch his head.

I said, "Are you ever busy in this shop? Does there ever come a time when you feel you would like to get your work done, instead of lingering over it and spinning it out for pure love of the thing?"

He did not appear to understand me. I said, "I met a man at your door a quarter of an hour ago, and we talked about these gloves that I want, and I told him all my ideas on the subject. He took me to your Mr Jansen, and Mr Jansen and I went over the whole business again. Now Mr Jansen leaves me with you – *you* who do not even know whether I want ladies' or gentlemen's gloves. Before I go over this story for the third time, I want to know whether you are the man who is going to serve me, or whether you are merely a listener, because personally I am tired of the subject?"

Well, this was the right man at last, and I got my gloves from him. But what is the explanation – what is the idea? I was in that shop from first to last five-and-thirty minutes.

And then a fool took me out the wrong way to show me a special line in sleeping-socks. I told him I was not requiring any. He said he didn't want me to buy, he only wanted me to see them. No wonder the drapers have had to start luncheon and tea-rooms. They'll fix up small furnished flats soon, where a woman can live for a week.'

I said it was very trying, shopping. I also said, as he invited me, and as he appeared determined to go on talking, that I would have a brandy-and-soda. We were in the smoke-room by this time.

'There ought to be an association,' he continued, 'a kind of clearing-house for the collection and distribution of Christmas presents. One would give them a list of the people from whom to collect presents, and of the people to whom to send. Suppose they collected on my account twenty Christmas presents, value, say, ten pounds, while on the other hand they sent out for me thirty presents at a cost of fifteen pounds. They would debit me with the balance of five pounds, together with a small commission. I should pay it cheerfully, and there would be no further trouble. Perhaps one might even make a profit. The idea might include birthdays and weddings. A firm would do the business thoroughly. They would see that all your friends paid up – I mean sent presents; and they would not forget to send to your most important relative. There is only one member of our family capable of leaving a shilling; and of course if I forget to send to any one it is to him. When I remember him I generally make a muddle of the business. Two years ago I gave him a bath – I don't mean I washed him – an india-rubber thing, that he could pack in his portmanteau. I thought he would find it useful for travelling. Would you believe it, he took it as a personal affront, and wouldn't speak to me for a month, the snuffy old idiot.'

'I suppose the children enjoy it,' I said.

'Enjoy what?' he asked.

'Why, Christmas,' I explained.

'I don't believe they do,' he snapped; 'nobody enjoys it. We excite them for three weeks beforehand, telling them what a good time they are going to have, over-feed them for two or three days, take them to something they do not want to see, but which we do, and then bully them for a fortnight to get them back into their normal condition. I was always taken to the Crystal Palace and Madame Tussaud's when I was a child, I remember. How I did hate that Crystal Palace! Aunt used to superintend. It was always a bitterly cold day, and we always got into the wrong train, and travelled half the day before we got there. We never had any dinner. It never occurs to a woman that anybody can want their meals while away from home. She seems to think that nature is in suspense from the time you leave the house till the time you get back to it. A bun and a glass of milk was her idea of lunch for a school-boy. Half her time was taken up in losing us, and the other half in slapping us when she had found us. The only thing we really enjoyed was the row with the cabman coming home.'

I rose to go.

'Then you won't join that symposium?' said B——. 'It would be an easy enough thing to knock off – 'Why Christmas should be abolished.'

'It sounds simple,' I answered. 'But how do you propose to abolish it?' The lady editor of an 'advanced' American magazine once set the discussion – 'Should sex be abolished?' and eleven ladies and gentlemen seriously argued the question.

'Leave it to die of inanition,' said B——; 'the first step is to arouse public opinion. Convince the public that it should be abolished.'

'But why should it be abolished?' I asked.

'Great Scott! man,' he exclaimed; 'don't you want it abolished?'

'I'm not sure that I do,' I replied.

'Not sure,' he retorted; 'you call yourself a journalist, and admit there is a subject under Heaven of which you are not sure!'

'It has come over me of late years,' I replied. 'It used not to be my failing, as you know.'

He glanced round to make sure we were out of earshot, then sunk his voice to a whisper.

'Between ourselves,' he said, 'I'm not so sure of everything myself as I used to be. Why is it?'

'Perhaps we are getting older,' I suggested.

He said – 'I started golf last year, and the first time I took the club in my hand I sent the ball a furlong. "It seems an easy game," I said to the man who was teaching me. "Yes, most people find it easy at the beginning," he replied drily. He was an old golfer himself; I thought he was jealous. I stuck well to the game, and for about three weeks I was immensely pleased with myself. Then, gradually, I began to find out the difficulties. I feel I shall never make a good player. Have you ever gone through that experience?'

'Yes,' I replied; 'I suppose that is the explanation. The game seems so easy at the beginning.'

I left him to his lunch, and strolled westward, musing on the time when I should have answered that question of his about Christmas, or any other question, off-hand. That good youth time when I knew everything, when life presented no problems, dangled no doubts before me!

In those days, wishful to give the world the benefit of my wisdom, and seeking for a candlestick wherefrom my brilliancy might be visible and helpful unto men, I arrived before a dingy portal in Chequers Street, St Luke's, behind which a conclave of young men, together with a few old enough to have known better, met every Friday evening for the purpose of discussing and arranging the affairs of the universe. 'Speaking members' were charged ten-and-sixpence per

annum, which must have worked out at an extremely moderate rate per word; and 'gentlemen whose subscriptions were more than three months in arrear' became, by Rule seven, powerless for good or evil. We called ourselves 'The Stormy Petrels', and, under the sympathetic shadow of those wings, I laboured two seasons towards the reformation of the human race; until, indeed, our treasurer, an earnest young man, and a tireless foe of all that was conventional, departed for the East, leaving behind him a balance sheet, showing that the club owed forty-two pounds fifteen and four-pence, and that the subscriptions for the current year, amounting to a little over thirty-eight pounds, had been 'carried forward', but as to where, the report afforded no indication. Whereupon our landlord, a man utterly without ideals, seized our furniture, offering to sell it back to us for fifteen pounds. We pointed out to him that this was an extravagant price, and tendered him five.

The negotiations terminated with ungentlemanly language on his part, and 'The Stormy Petrels' scattered, never to be foregathered together again above the troubled waters of humanity. Now-a-days, listening to the feeble plans of modern reformers, I cannot help but smile, remembering what was done in Chequers Street, St Luke's, in an age when Mrs Grundy still gave the law to literature, while yet the British matron was the guide to British art. I am informed that there is abroad the question of abolishing the House of Lords! Why, 'The Stormy Petrels' abolished the aristocracy and the Crown in one evening, and then only adjourned for the purpose of appointing a committee to draw up and have ready a Republican Constitution by the following Friday evening. They talk of Empire lounges! We closed the doors of every music-hall in London eighteen years ago by twenty-nine votes to seventeen. They had a patient hearing, and were ably defended; but we found that the tendency of such amuse-

ments was anti-progressive, and against the best interests of an intellectually advancing democracy. I met the mover of the condemnatory resolution at the old 'Pav' the following evening, and we continued the discussion over a bottle of Bass. He strengthened his argument by persuading me to sit out the whole of the three songs sung by the 'Lion Comique'; but I subsequently retorted successfully, by bringing under his notice the dancing of a lady in blue tights and flaxen hair. I forget her name, but never shall I cease to remember her exquisite charm and beauty. Ah, me! how charming and how beautiful 'artistes' were in those golden days! Whence have they vanished? Ladies in blue tights and flaxen hair dance before my eyes today, but move me not, unless it be towards boredom. Where be the tripping witches of twenty years ago, whom to see once was to dream of for a week, to touch whose white hand would have been joy, to kiss whose red lips would have been to foretaste Heaven. I heard only the other day that the son of an old friend of mine had secretly married a lady from the front row of the ballet, and involuntarily I exclaimed, 'Poor devil!' There was a time when my first thought would have been, 'Lucky beggar! is he worthy of her?' For then the ladies of the ballet were angels. How could one gaze at them – from the shilling pit – and doubt it? They danced to keep a widowed mother in comfort, or to send a younger brother to school. Then they were glorious creatures a young man did well to worship; but now-a-days –

It is an old jest. The eyes of youth see through rose-tinted glasses. The eyes of age are dim behind smoke-clouded specta-cles. My flaxen friend, you are not the angel I dreamed you, nor the exceptional sinner some would paint you; but under your feathers, just a woman – a bundle of follies and failings, tied up with some sweetness and strength. You keep a brougham I am sure you cannot afford on your thirty shillings a week. There are ladies I know, in Mayfair, who have paid an

extravagant price for theirs. You paint and you dye, I am told: it is even hinted you pad. Don't we all of us deck ourselves out in virtues that are not our own? When the paint and powder, my sister, is stripped both from you and from me, we shall know which of us is entitled to look down on the other in scorn.

Forgive me, gentle Reader, for digressing. The lady led me astray. I was speaking of 'The Stormy Petrels', and of the reforms they accomplished, which were many. We abolished, I remember, capital punishment and war; we were excellent young men at heart. Christmas we reformed altogether, along with Bank Holidays, by a majority of twelve. I never recollect any proposal to abolish anything ever being lost when put to the vote. There were few things that we 'Stormy Petrels' did not abolish. We attacked Christmas on grounds of expediency, and killed it by ridicule. We exposed the hollow mockery of Christmas sentiment; we abused the indigestible Christmas dinner, the tiresome Christmas party, the silly Christmas pantomime. Our funny member was side-splitting on the subject of Christmas Waits; our social reformer bitter upon Christmas drunkenness; our economist indignant upon Christmas charities. Only one argument of any weight with us was advanced in favour of the festival, and that was our leading cynic's suggestion that it was worth enduring the miseries of Christmas, to enjoy the soul-satisfying comfort of the after reflection that it was all over, and could not occur again for another year.

But since those days when I was prepared to put this old world of ours to rights upon all matters, I have seen many sights and heard many sounds, and I am not quite so sure as I once was that my particular views are the only possible correct ones. Christmas seems to me somewhat meaningless; but I have looked through windows in poverty-stricken streets, and have seen dingy parlours gay with many chains of coloured paper. They stretched from corner to corner of the smoke-

Buildings all familiar to Jerome but now gone from Walsall's
Church Hill

grimed ceiling, they fell in clumsy festoons from the cheap gasalier, they framed the fly-blown mirror and the tawdry pictures; and I know tired hands and eyes worked many hours to fashion and fix those foolish chains, saying, 'It will please him – she will like to see the room look pretty;' and as I have looked at them they have grown, in some mysterious manner, beautiful to me. The gaudy-coloured child and dog irritates me, I confess; but I have watched a grimy, inartistic personage, smoothing it affectionately with toil-stained hand, while eager faces crowded round to admire and wonder at its blatant crudity. It hangs to this day in its cheap frame above the chimney-piece, the one bright spot relieving those damp-stained walls; dull eyes stare and stare again at it, catching a vista, through its flashy tints, of the far-off land of art. Christmas Waits annoy me, and I yearn to throw open the window and fling coal at them – as once from the window of a high flat in Chelsea I did. I doubted their being genuine Waits. I was inclined to the opinion they were young men seeking excuse for making a noise. One of them appeared to know a hymn with a chorus, another played the concertina, while a third accompanied with a step dance. Instinctively I felt no respect for them; they disturbed me in my work, and the desire grew upon me to injure them. It occurred to me it would be good sport if I turned out the light, softly opened the window, and threw coal at them. It would be impossible for them to tell from which window in the block the coal came, and thus subsequent unpleasantness would be avoided. They were a compact little group, and with average luck I was bound to hit one of them.

I adopted the plan. I could not see them very clearly. I aimed rather at the noise; and I had thrown about twenty choice lumps without effect, and was feeling somewhat discouraged, when a yell, followed by language singularly inappropriate to the season, told me that Providence had aided my

arm. The music ceased suddenly, and the party dispersed, apparently in high glee – which struck me as curious.

One man I noticed remained behind. He stood under the lamp-post, and shook his fist at the block generally.

'Who threw that lump of coal?' he demanded in stentorian tones.

To my horror, it was the voice of the man at Eighty-eight, an Irish gentleman, a journalist like myself. I saw it all, as the unfortunate hero always exclaims, too late, in the play. He – number Eighty-eight – also disturbed by the noise, had evidently gone out to expostulate with the rioters. Of course my lump of coal had hit him – him the innocent, the peaceful (up till then), the virtuous. That is the justice Fate deals out to us mortals here below. There were ten to fourteen young men in that crowd, each one of whom fully deserved that lump of coal; he, the one guiltless, got it – seemingly, so far as the dim light from the gas lamp enabled me to judge, full in the eye.

As the block remained silent in answer to his demand, he crossed the road and mounted the stairs. On each landing he stopped and shouted –

'Who threw that lump of coal. I want the man who threw that lump of coal. Out you come.'

Now a good man in my place would have waited till number Eighty-eight arrived on his landing, and then, throwing open the door, would have said with manly candour –

'*I* threw that lump of coal. I was –,' He would not have got further, because at that point, I feel confident, number Eighty-eight would have punched his head. There would have been an unseemly fracas on the staircase, to the annoyance of all the other tenants; and later, there would have issued a summons and a cross-summons. Angry passions would have been roused, bitter feeling engendered which might have lasted for years.

I do not pretend to be a good man. I doubt if the pretence

would be of any use were I to try: I am not a sufficiently good actor. I said to myself, as I took off my boots in the study, preparatory to retiring to my bedroom – 'Number Eighty-eight is evidently not in a frame of mind to listen to my story. It will be better to let him shout himself cool; after which he will return to his own flat, bathe his eye, and obtain some refreshing sleep. In the morning, when we shall probably meet as usual on our way to Fleet Street, I will refer to the incident casually, and sympathize with him. I will suggest to him the truth – that in all probability some fellow-tenant, irritated also by the noise, had aimed coal at the Waits, hitting him instead by a regrettable but pure accident. With tact I may even be able to make him see the humour of the incident. Later on, in March or April, choosing my moment with judgment, I will, perhaps, confess that I was that fellow-tenant, and over a friendly brandy-and-soda we will laugh the whole trouble away.'

As a matter of fact, that is what happened. Said number Eighty-eight – he was a big man, as good a fellow at heart as ever lived, but impulsive – 'Damned lucky for you, old man, you did not tell me at the time.'

'I felt', I replied, 'instinctively that it was a case for delay.'

There are times when one should control one's passion for candour; and as I was saying, Christmas Waits excite no emotion in my breast save that of irritation. But I have known 'Hark, the herald angels sing,' wheezily chanted by fog-filled throats, and accompanied, hopelessly out of time, by a cornet and a flute, bring a great look of gladness to a work-worn face. To her it was a message of hope and love, making the hard life taste sweet. The mere thought of family gatherings, so customary at Christmas time, bores us superior people; but I think of an incident told me by a certain man, a friend of mine. One Christmas, my friend, visiting in the country, came face to face with a woman whom in town he had often

met amid very different surroundings. The door of the little farmhouse was open; she and an older woman were ironing at a table, and as her soft white hands passed to and fro, folding and smoothing the rumpled heap, she laughed and talked, concerning simple homely things. My friend's shadow fell across her work, and she, looking up, their eyes met; but her face said plainly, 'I do not know you here, and here you do not know me. Here I am a woman loved and respected.' My friend passed in and spoke to the older woman, the wife of one of his host's tenants, and she turned towards, and introduced the younger – 'My daughter, sir. We do not see her very often. She is in a place in London, and cannot get away. But she always spends a few days with us at Christmas.'

'It is the season for family re-unions,' answered my friend with just the suggestion of a sneer, for which he hated himself.

'Yes, sir,' said the woman, not noticing; 'she has never missed her Christmas with us, have you, Bess?'

'No, mother,' replied the girl simply, and bent her head again over her work.

So for these few days every year this woman left her furs and jewels, her fine clothes and dainty foods, behind her, and lived for a little space with what was clean and wholesome. It was the one anchor holding her to womanhood; and one likes to think that it was, perhaps, in the end strong enough to save her from the drifting waters. All which arguments in favour of Christmas and of Christmas customs are, I admit, purely sentimental ones, but I have lived long enough to doubt whether sentiment has not its legitimate place in the economy of life.

from

Bilston Wesleyan Methodism

JOHN FREEMAN

*Methodism thrived within the Black Country largely thanks
to the efforts of John Wesley who at first met with much
opposition. Once established, local congregations usually
maintained a lasting loyalty to their chapel, as in this case of
Bilston where the local historian compiled a book of 'notes of its
origin and progress' for the centenary celebrations of November
1923.*

1844. – The Christmas Tea Meeting had so grown in favour
that more than 500 tickets were sold this year; and the after-
meeting was to be held in the Chapel, when Rev. Dr Bunting,
President of the Conference, and Rev. Dr R. Newton, the sec-
retary, were to attend and give suitable addresses.

The Church decorations were to be far from severe. In front
of the pulpit, which was to be suitably draped, they arranged
to place a large portrait of Wesley. The ornamentation was to
consist of two transparent paintings, six pictures in oils lent
by Mrs Howell, ornate embellishments on the chandeliers,
and a tasteful distribution of evergreens. The ladies were
invited to bring their best china, and numbers of men were

called upon to play the part of conductors to the various tables, and to render all necessary chivalrous service to the ladies. This Tea Meeting held its charm until about the seventies. Many still living will recall its outstanding features; the tremendous loads of holly and bay, which, under the hand of Mr B. Beebee and his helpers, transformed the room into an arcadia; the fussy, but not unbeautiful, balloon-like shades upon the pendants, and the deft and variegated ribbons woven overhead into a riot of colour; and most interesting of all, three Transparencies which hung on the wall over the platform; number one representing the Chapel when first built, and having the inscription:

'Who hath despised the day of small things?'

The second one showing the building of the middle period was inscribed:

'Hitherto the Lord hath helped us.'

And the last one depicting the latest development bore the triumphant passage:

'What hath God wrought!'

The first and second of these paintings apparently were the property in 1844 of the widow of Mr Joseph Howell, and there is little doubt, as he was a clever painter, of their being his handy-work.

The third one, added a few years later, was probably a product of the art of Mr B. Beebee. After the discontinuance of the Tea Meeting the pictures were stored away, and in some strange way disappeared.

The catering was a strong feature. We are not aware that the tea was ever made pungent, as at some other meeting in the town, by the addition of certain seductive flavours; but we know the tables were loaded in a sumptuous manner. Each table was provided by a lady at her own cost, who had a free hand in the choice of viands. Naturally rivalry was keen, and many tables were favoured above others. That this kind of

competition was spiritually healthy we should hesitate to affirm.

However, the meeting was a great function; we shall never forget its crowds, its happy enthusiasm, and its memorable speeches. Year after year Rev. H.W. Holland, one of Birmingham's galaxy of public men, in which George Dawson and R.W. Dale figured, lifted the meeting by the sheer force of his mind on to a high level, creating a spirit that was a tonic to the whole Church. It should not be forgotten that for many years the meeting produced a substantial financial sum for the work of the Sunday Schools.

Black Country Pantomime

CHARLES HATTON

As a freelance journalist Charles Hatton became very familiar with many aspects of the social and industrial life of the Black Country and its people. With many of his 'sketches' appearing in Birmingham newspapers he omitted the exact Black Country dialect which he felt 'indigestible in print even to those who are familiar with it'.

'Line up for the walk-down!' whispers the stage manager hoarsely. 'Ready? Right!'

Down they come to the strains of the finale. Chorus first, then the minor principals, speciality acts, comedian, principal girl and boy.

Everybody is singing at the top of their voices; the applause sweeps from the auditorium in waves of growing intensity over which the band, going all out, is only just heard.

The curtain swings down. Then up again. More applause, strident whistles and cheers. Bouquets and presents are loaded upon the company. And everybody sings the National Anthem.

Then the curtain makes its final descent upon this touring pantomime. The show is over until next year.

Throughout this last performance, costumes have been hastily packed into hampers as they have been discarded, properties stowed away, scenery neatly stacked ready for the railway wagon which will call presently to convey it to the station, and so to its storing place in some distant warehouse.

The Babes are clinging to Robin Hood, sniffing dismally, while even the doughty Robin's eyes are suspiciously moist.

'Robin, I don't want to leave you,' cries the girl Babe.

'Same here, dear. I could do with another week's salary as well as the next!'

Robin tries to sound hard-boiled, but there is a noticeable creak in 'his' voice. Robin has grown very fond of these youngsters in the month they have been constantly thrown together.

Meanwhile, some of the local lads have called round at the stage door to say good-bye, or escort home the recipients of their presents.

The stage manager scowls at them, but they cheerfully ignore him. He has been their arch-enemy all the week, and can hardly be blamed, for there is no doubt that 'followers' who expect to stand at the side of the stage do interfere with the smooth running of a show.

He has some difficulty in asserting his authority, for many rules go by the board in small town pantomime, and, with few understudies available, one has to be careful in offending principals who are well-nigh impossible to replace at short notice.

Up in the dressing rooms the farewells continue, interspersed with rapid packing, rescuing odd bits of greasepaint, cleaning off tonight's mask of paint and powder, separating one's own property from that supplied by the management.

At last everything is straightened out; the dressing rooms are empty save for odd bits of rubbish.

The garish bulbs around the mirrors are switched out, doors are slammed, slightly hysterical voices scream exuberant adieux along the echoing corridors.

Under a single pilot light, nothing could be less glamorous than the deserted stage, with its scenery stacked against the grimy walls, and a thin film of dust still visible in the rapidly chilling atmosphere.

'Well,' murmurs the principal boy, as she takes a last look round to make sure she has forgotten nothing, 'that's another year gone. I wonder if I'll ever get out of these mouldy shows and reach Drury Lane.'

Not much sentiment there, but she can't afford to stand on her dignity and refuse fifteen good pounds a week.

She makes her way up the stone steps and out of the stage door, catching up with a small party of fellow artistes on their noisy way back to the 'digs'.

In the narrow lane outside the stage door the railway dray is patiently waiting.

The driver looks rather more wide awake than usual, despite the lateness of the hour. He doesn't often 'click' for a job like this, which is certainly a novelty compared with his usual work of conveying bales of goods and lumps of metal to and from the goods yards.

Queuing for the panto treat at Dudley Hippodrome in 1956

Back in their 'digs', various members of the company are holding impromptu parties.

In first-rate pantomime the management usually gives a large party to which the whole cast is invited. But the 'governor' of this particular crowd has a reputation for meanness, though he has made over a thousand pounds for this company alone. Hasn't he spent the greater part of the evening trying to persuade them to buy the blocks of their Press photos?

So the artistes are left to devise their own humble celebrations, which invariably take the form of ham and eggs, followed by any drinks they have had the forethought to procure.

They review the incidents of the tour, the 'digs' they have suffered, the Sunday journeys with their inevitable wait at Crewe, the minor scandals and romances in the company, the

conceit of the comedian, the stage manager's temper, and lots more besides.

Though many of them express their intention of catching an early train next morning, no one thinks of going to bed before two o'clock after further farewells. Eventually, the landlady is able to compose herself for sleep with a sigh of relief.

Next morning the company will scatter to all corners of the country. Some will return to London, where they will continue the rounds of the film and variety agents in search of work. Others realise that this is useless, and live quietly at home until Easter, when they emerge once more to meet the demand for concert party artistes.

The principal boy and baron, who are husband and wife, will return to their homely little inn, which has been left in charge of relatives.

So this happy-go-lucky family breaks up. For several weeks they have shared hardships and joys, suffered under the biting tongue of the producer and stage manager, nursed each other's minor ailments, revelled in the applause of thousands of excited children and adults. The odds are heavily against them ever meeting again.

In addition to earning very good money – pantomime salaries are higher than in any other show – they have the satisfaction of knowing they have brought happiness to many a childish heart, which will be eagerly remembered for many months.

'Good-bye dear, see you in the next pantomime,' they shout to each other optimistically as their trains move out on Sunday morning.

Tomorrow night, the dressing rooms will be empty, the stage once more obscured by the vast screen, the talkie loudspeakers booming away merrily.

And pantomime will be relegated to the land of memories.

Christmas Memories

PAT WARNER

Born in a lock cottage on the Worcester and Birmingham Canal, Pat Warner experienced a harsh childhood with the early death of her mother, brother and some of her sisters. Despite this the lock-keeper's daughter found 'nothing to compare with a childhood Christmas' vividly remembered during a visit to her relatives in Wolverhampton.

The Winter of 1928, it just snowed and snowed. We didn't see the milkman or the postman for a number of weeks. Somehow, this seemed fairly normal in those days and we were always well prepared.

The snow would pile up along the towing path, two or three feet high – sometimes higher. And it was cold. So cold at night that it would freeze the contents of the chamber pot under the bed! I would keep warm with a hot brick wrapped in a piece of flannel. But what a pretty sight was all that snow! Clean, white snow, not dirty, slushy stuff. The sun shining and long icicles hanging from the lock gates. If you looked across the Reservoir from the back bedroom window, you might catch a glimpse of some wild creature which had dared venture out. You might even see a red squirrel, sitting in one of the trees, holding a hazel nut between his front paws.

Christmas canal study by Alan Ledbury

I knew that if the weather didn't improve, we would be unable to visit my Aunt and Uncle for Christmas. They lived, I thought, on the other side of the world, but it was only Wolverhampton. All that long distance was a great adventure for me. It began with a two-mile walk to the bus stop at Tardebigge. The fare from there to Bromsgrove was 5d (2p). We would then travel to Stourbridge – another shilling (5p) – and from there to the LMS station at Wolverhampton – one more shilling. This would take most of a day. On reaching journey's end, the Wolverhampton snow was all wet and dirty, not like the nice clean snow I was used to.

Most of Christmas Eve was passed in taking trams to visit the shops. What a good thing I liked buses and trams, because not all the dolls and sweets in England would have persuaded me to get into a car. I was terrified of motor cars! The large stores in town stayed open until 8 o'clock at night and I would be able to buy all my Christmas presents with the 2s 6d (12½p) I had saved.

We would return to my Aunt's house for supper and go to the midnight service at the huge church in nearby Cannock. There would be a big choir, a lovely crib and (as I then described it) the man with the flat hat would swing the innocents around! The smell of the incense would stay in my nostrils for days. After we left church, my Aunt and Uncle would curse and argue all the way home.

Here, at my Aunt's, I would sleep in a folding chair. I lay awake for hours, waiting for Father Christmas to come down the chimney. Somehow, I always missed him. I had the same presents in my stocking each year: a large coloured play ball, a sugar pig, an orange and one bright new shining penny.

Christmas in Wolverhampton meant more to me than anything else in the world. For once, there would be water from the tap by the sink; gas light in the kitchen to show me the way across the yard to the WC outside; a gas stove in the kitchen on which to boil the kettle . . . all this was achieved at the turn of a switch. The mantle in the light globe made a funny hissing sound, quite warm and homely. So different to the lamplight at Tardebigge. A gas light glowed in the street just outside the house and friendly noises could be heard from the shunting yard at the nearby railway station.

Aunt Polly had no children and was very house proud. Everything clean and bright, scrubbed and polished, a place for everything and everything in its place. A cheerful coal fire threw out ample heat from a black-leaded grate that shone like glass. So shiny that I could see the reflections of my red

cheeks. The only time when Aunt Polly wasn't working was when she was eating, sleeping, praying or playing cards.

There were always nice things to eat with little luxuries like sago pudding. On Christmas morning it was cold boiled ham for breakfast. Uncle worked for the Railway and was 'rich'! Afterwards, we dressed in our Sunday Best to attend the Christmas Morning service. But first, always on a Christmas Morning, without fail, my Aunt would scrub the back yard. Down she went on her hands and knees and scrubbed and scrubbed. Meanwhile, my 'rich' Uncle became madder and madder, shouting and blaspheming and then hoping that the Good Lord would forgive him.

If we were lucky, we might get our Christmas dinner about 3.00p.m. I just couldn't wait for dinner to be cleared away because I knew that afterwards the grown-ups would play cards so they wouldn't need me around. That could only mean one thing:

'Put little Pat into the parlour. There's a nice fire. She can amuse herself.'

A lovely fire cast its shadow on the parlour ceiling. It was the only day of the year that this room was open to the public apart from weddings and funerals. The 'holy of holies' shone brighter than the Eastern Star! Cards finished, my Uncle could settle down for the great moment he had been waiting for: a sing song around the piano. The walls of 30, Smestow Street, just off the Cannock Road, would ring with the rendering of fine old Victorian Carols. My favourite was *The Mistletoe Bough* by Thomas Haynes Bayly.

> The mistletoe hung in the castle hall.
> The holly branch shone on the old oak wall.
> The Baron's retainers were blithe and gay
> While keeping their Christmas holiday.
> The Baron beheld with a fatherly pride

His beautiful child, young Lovell's bride.
She, with her bright eyes, seemed to be
The star of that goodly company.
Oh, the mistletoe bough,
Oh, the mistletoe bough.

Uncle Dick was a good pianist and that never-to-be-forgotten carol made a perfect Christmas. We went home the day after Boxing Day.

I didn't have a Christmas tree, either at home or at my Aunt's. A holly bush would be hung from a large hook in the ceiling at home, provided that the home-cured bacon had first been removed. This top, taken from a holly tree, was a pretty sight, a bow of tinsel, a pink sugar pig and a white sugar mouse being the only decorations. But it filled the house with the spirit and magic of Christmas. I knew that the little pig, with his friend the mouse, would afterwards be returned to their paper wrappings for next Christmas . . . and the next . . . and the next. Eventually, they were so old, worn and dusty they were almost beyond recognition. I never knew what happened to them.

There is nothing to compare with a childhood Christmas. The waking at some unearthly hour for that wonderful moment when you looked for your presents. They were always there. The great preparations beforehand like sitting up through the night to boil the Christmas puddings in the copper. Mince pies were the size of saucers, covered in caster sugar and often washed down with a glass of Father's homemade 'poison'. It was an adventure to go tramping through the snow to gather the holly, ivy and mistletoe from some secret place. The snow was as fine and white as the icing on the cake. And you must never forget to make a wish whilst stirring the Christmas puddings.

A Tame Valley canal scene with fun for the children

Childhood Christmas treats left a great impression in my mind. The magic of hanging up a pillowcase, the feel of the sugar pig and the orange lying hidden in one corner and most of all that wonderful faith in Father Christmas.

Home from Wolverhampton, it was strange to lie in my own bed again and to listen to the weird sounds of the cut instead of the rattling trams going up the Cannock Road. Father, too, enjoyed these Christmas treats as much as I did. Before we went away he would read Dickens' *Christmas Carol* to me, the story of Scrooge and the ghosts and the sad little Tiny Tim. He was probably glad to get away from our house in case he, too, might see the spirits of Christmases past.

A Black Country Christmas

Some of my thoughts of those long ago Christmases I have put into verse:

> Always on a Christmas morn
> I remember bygone years.
> The music and the singing:
> The laughter and the tears.
>
> A musty smell of unused rooms
> Still lingers in my nose.
> The mistletoe bough, the holly bunch
> With the lovely Christmas Rose.
>
> The choir boys and the lovely crib.
> The hymns and carols gay.
> The smell of incense in the church:
> This was my Christmas Day.
>
> The shunting in the goods yard.
> Trams rattling on their way.
> All these memories I hold dear:
> They made my Christmas Day.
>
> Gas lights hissing in the street.
> Houses standing in a row.
> The sounds of weary trudging feet,
> Quietly muffled by the snow.
>
> Anecdotes of Christmas
> Which will never go away.
> Nostalgic echoes from the past
> Of every Christmas Day.

from

Portrait of Clare

FRANCIS BRETT YOUNG

*In his numerous novels, many with a West Midlands flavour,
Francis Brett Young makes little attempt to disguise an
original placename – here in this extract Wolverbury is
Wolverhampton, and North Bromwich is obvious! Born in
Halesowen (Halesby in his novels) where his father was
medical officer of health, Brett Young trained as a doctor before
pursuing a writing career.*

At Christmas time the fierce rhythm of this too-rapid life was
broken by a visit to Stourford. Aunt Cathie also was invited,
but refused the benefit of any concession on 'that woman's'
part. She could never forgive the Stourford drawing-room for
being what it was. As a protest against it she intensified the
deepness of her mourning, appearing, on the day of Clare's
departure, in a hot aura of crape. Clare gathered that Mr
Wilburn had approved her attitude; for though his visits to
Pen House had ceased at the time of her engagement, Aunt
Cathie continued to write to him enormous letters, marked
'confidential', which she formally sealed in Clare's presence, as
though she thought that they would be steamed open in the
kitchen.

'There's no reason why you shouldn't leave me for
Christmas, Clare,' she said. 'I am used to being alone. The

doctor always despised women who were without resources. I shall read *Romola* – that will be most appropriate, since you are going to Italy so soon – and I shall finish all those cambric chemises. I've told Thirza to buy a chicken. The very thought of cold turkey makes me ill. They're such immense birds.'

'I shall be back again in three days, dearest,' Clare assured her.

'No doubt you will have a gay time,' said Aunt Cathie dolefully. 'A quiet person like myself would be totally out of place. Besides, I suppose I must get used to being without you. I don't suppose I shall see much of Thirza. I've allowed her to invite her friend to dine with her, and Ellen, of course, will go home to her parents on Christmas Day.'

By this time Clare had deliberately steeled herself against these harrowing resignations. She knew that Aunt Cathie would be much happier in the company of George Eliot than in that of George Hingston. She kissed her good-bye with an untroubled face, and the embrace which Aunt Cathie returned was surprising in its warmth and tenderness.

Even on this occasion the approach to Stourford seemed formidable; there was no knowing with what new brilliant variation of the offensive Lady Hingston might not confound her; for since the day of the wedding had been fixed they had only met among the crowds which ebbed and flowed through the hall at Stourford like people at a railway station. Then Lady Hingston had treated her with a sort of gracious contempt, acknowledging her presence as a harmless necessary evil; now she might make a final protest against the evil's necessity.

She did not. The Hingstons were people who, apart from its religious significance, took Christmas seriously. The festival had feudal aspects that they were anxious to preserve. It gave them a chance of showing their tenants the benignity of the old regime – new style – at its best; and the process was so exacting that Lady Hingston's energies were absorbed in it.

She was too busy to think of quarrelling with anybody, and the addition of a new helper, even in the questionable shape of Clare, was welcome to her.

On Christmas Eve they made a feast for servants and tenants in the long music-room. After dinner the room was cleared for dancing, and Clare found herself revolving solemnly in the arms of Mr Parker. Mr Parker breathed noisily through his nose, for, in ordinary life, such rapid movements were not compatible with his dignity. His eyes were busy all the time watching for any signs of impropriety in the behaviour of his staff. He bore Clare round the room as carefully as if she had been an entrée. From first to last his lips uttered no word; and Clare was almost thankful that they didn't, so convinced was she that, if words came, they must take the shape of, 'Ice pudding or meringue, Miss?'

Marguerite did not dance. Not even with Ralph. No doubt she felt that knowledge of her dissolute nationality might tempt the footmen to unseemly advances. She sat upright and superb, an emblem of invitation and discouragement, unconscious of the sprig of mistletoe that hung above her head. Vivien and Lady Hingston were everywhere, like bright birds thridding the constrained and sombre company. The sullen loveliness of Eleanor's eyes followed them wherever they went. She was more lifelessly beautiful that night, Clare thought, than ever before. Her two children, little Harold and Enid, came romping to her knee, but not even they could bring a breath of life into her face. It seemed incredible that anything so vital as they could have been born of Eleanor's coldness. And like a soul strayed out of some distant circle of purgatory into another, Sir Joseph Hingston moved shyly round the room's outer edge, always wavering toward the door by which he might have escaped, always recalled to his melancholy duty by his wife's black eyes.

Suddenly, when she least expected it, he threw himself

upon the mercy of Clare. It was embarrassing, for she had never been alone with him before, and on her former visit he had not seemed to be aware of her existence. He sat with one leg awkwardly cocked above the other, his bald head sunken between his shoulders, and began to talk in a low monotone about her grandfather. The subject carried him back to the days before the overwhelming prosperity of Wolverbury. He spoke of them almost with regret.

'We had a neat little works in those days,' he said, 'and if it hadn't been for the boom that followed the Franco-Prussian war I expect we should be there still. That war was a marvellous thing for the Midlands. It made our friend Walter Willis, as well as me. War's a grand thing for iron. But Walter Willis' – he shook his head – 'there's something wrong with him. He's a clever fellow in his way, is Willis; but his head's not steady enough; he can't stand oats, as our Ralph would put it. I don't say that Mawne isn't a fine concern to look at. It's all right on paper, my dear. But when the slump comes, as it's bound to, folk like Walter Willis'll have to put on their thinking-caps.'

He lowered his voice to a whisper, almost as if he were making confidences to a fellow iron-master. Clare listened intently, though she could not understand half of what he was saying. He began to talk of the new Sedgebury Main Colliery, the masterpiece of the red-bearded Furnival whom Clare had met at Stourford two months before.

'Walter Willis has gone into that like a mad bull,' he said, 'and our George is every bit as wild about it as he is. I'm chairman of the company. I couldn't get out of it. You see they wanted my name. Well, well, they can have it. But when it comes to money . . . I'm not a geologist, my dear. Fortunately, we're in a position to pay for the best brains in that line, the same as any other. Kneeworth – he's the professor at Astill's College in North Bromwich, you know –

Kneeworth says Furnival's right. Well, maybe; I don't know. But one thing I do know, and that is that my old grandfather worked down that pit hewing coal for thirty years, and I can recollect sitting by him, just as it might be you, my dear, and hearing him say: "You mind my words; I can smell water in that pit," and whenever I hear Furnival speechifying these words come back. George says I've got water on the brain. Maybe he's right, but I've got summat else as well, as we used to say.'

He stopped and stared in front of him into the glazed eyes of Parker leading a quadrille. Then, clumsily, he patted Clare's hand.

'I'm glad to have had this bit of a chat with you,' he said. 'I can see that you've got a heart, Clare, and our Ralph's a lucky chap. He's right to have cut himself out of Wolverbury too. He's not built for it any more than young Willis is, though his dad won't see it. That's what I meant just now. D'you see? No, we've no room for passengers in concerns like ours. What's more, you've helped me to make up my mind about this business of Furnival's. It's extraordinary how a quiet talk puts your ideas in order.'

His hand went fumbling to his waistcoat pocket, as though his mind, concentrated on Wolverbury, grudged the energy necessary to direct his fingers. He pulled out a folded piece of paper and slipped it into her palm.

'I made this out for you this morning,' he said, 'and you may as well have it before twelve as after. It's just a trifle to buy a bit of hair-ribbon with, as they say. Don't lose it, there's a good girl! And now I think you might give your father-in-law a kiss under the mistletoe.'

Clare did so willingly. Before that evening she had always thought of Sir Joseph as remote, and possibly unfriendly, so detached from all humanity had he seemed. Now she realised that the Sir Joseph of Stourford and the Sir Joseph of

Snow in the early 1900s covering the former thatch on the lodge to
Tettenhall Wood House

Wolverbury were different beings, and that when he was torn
away from his works he left the greater part of his personality
behind. In all the long meanderings of their talk the smaller
fragment had been straining away from the music-room in the
direction of its complement. Thanks to her silence it had
almost succeeded in its quest. He kissed her; even his kiss was
curiously impersonal;. and then, fired with unusual courage,
he hurried from the room. Vivien pounced upon Clare and
dragged her into a set of lancers. Later, when she had time to
look at the paper which he had put into her hand, she found
that it was a cheque for a thousand pounds.

Nor was this astounding document the only one that excited her during her stay at Stourford. Ever since the announce-
ment of the wedding, presents had been pouring in; for trade,

in the North Bromwich district was booming, and most of its wealthier manufacturers were eager to stand well with the Hingstons. Ralph took their generosity for granted. He had been brought up in a house where luxurious possessions counted for little; but to Clare the accumulations of presents that blew into the library like a snowdrift from every quarter of the compass were almost terrifying; they seemed to turn her wedding, which hitherto she had considered as an affair that concerned nobody but themselves, into a public event. It made her thank Heaven that the actual ceremony, which was to take place at Wychbury and from Pen House, would be more in keeping with her modesty.

On Christmas Day the family dined in state. They played the game of peace and goodwill so effectively that if Parker had not been in their service for years he might easily have imagined that they were as united as they appeared to be. They all drank Clare's health and Ralph's in a magnum of Pommery: a dangerous experiment; for Lady Hingston was already reacting from the democratic good-humours of the night before, and alcohol, in any form, was apt to make her irritable. At once she began to lay down her own law on the subject of Eleanor's nurse and the conduct of Eleanor's children; her black eyes flashed; her accusations became more and more outrageous; it was as though she were giving Clare an exhibition of the kind of thing that she would have to put up with when she and Ralph were married. But an instrument keener than Lady Hingston's tongue was needed to pierce the apathy of Eleanor; for lack of fuel her violence blazed away as harmlessly as a fuse that stops short of detonation; and Vivien, dashing in gallantly to the rescue with some calculated stupidity, saved her mother's face.

It was a dull evening; for though they pretended that they were enjoying themselves, they were all too familiar and too individual to find amusement in each others' company. No doubt it was partly this lack of communal interest that had

compelled them to make Stourford the open house which it was. When the children had been packed off to bed, and the effects of the champagne had evaporated, long periods of silence fell upon them. Little by little the artificial bonds were loosened and the company began to split up into its natural grouping. Lady Hingston took out a pack of patience cards. George and Sir Joseph edged away towards the library, where the cigars were kept. Vivien and Eleanor sat talking with voices lowered for fear of disturbing Lady Hingston's concentration on her cards. Ralph leaned over Clare's shoulder from behind and whispered her away into the morning-room. As they stole out together Clare felt as furtive as if she had pilfered the drawing-room silver; but when they passed the card-table Lady Hingston looked up with a smile so charming that she was compelled, by a sudden impulse, to stoop and kiss her.

from

The Journal of Francis Asbury

Known as the 'Prophet of the Long Road' — 275,000 miles travelled on horseback — Francis Asbury from Great Barr took up John Wesley's challenge for preachers to go to America. Asbury's loyalty to America during the War of Independence

earned him a place on the roll of the new nation's founding
fathers and it was on Christmas Eve 1784 that he became the
first Bishop of the American Methodist Episcopal Church.
Today the Church is America's largest – a fitting tribute to
Asbury's pioneering spirit.

South Carolina
December 1792

Sunday, 23. We rode this evening twenty miles to Mr Blakeney's: the rain caught us in the woods, and we were steeped. Arriving, we found a good house, table, and bed, which was some relief to weather-beaten pilgrims.

Christmas Eve. We rode in the rain twenty-five miles to our kind brother Horton's, and found many people had gathered.

Christmas Day. Although the weather was cold and damp, and unhealthy, with signs of snow, we rode forty-five miles to dear brother Rembert's – kind and good, rich and liberal, who has done more for the poor Methodists than any man in South Carolina. The Lord grant that he, with his whole household, may find mercy in that day.

Wednesday, 26. Preached at quarterly meeting on 1 Peter iv, 13. I was pleased to hear the young men exhort and sing after sacrament. I felt uncommonly melted – tears involuntarily burst from my eyes. God was there.

Thursday, 27. I had a long, cold ride of forty-five miles to brother Bowman's, near Santee. I was overtaken on my way by rain mingled with hail which ended in snow, covering the ground six or eight inches deep. The unfinished state of the houses, lying on the floor, thin clothing, and inclement weather keep me in a state of indisposition.

Friday, 28. We had to cross Santee, and ride thirty-five miles to dear sister Browning's. The weather still very cold.

Saturday, 29. Rode thirty-three miles to Charleston, and

Old Chapel Farm, Smethwick – a typical old-world farm familiar to
Asbury from his blacksmithing days

found our little flock in peace, and a small revival amongst
them.

Mr Hammett has raised a grand house, and has written an
appeal to the British conference. He represents Dr. Coke as a
sacrilegious tyrant and murderer. I have no doubt but the
Doctor will be able to make good his cause. As to Hammett,
time will show the man and the people who have made lies
their refuge.

Sunday, 30. Brother Isaac Smith preached in the forenoon.
In the afternoon I said a little on Isaiah ix, 6, 7. The blacks
were hardly restrained from crying out aloud. O that God
would bless the wild and wicked inhabitants of this city! I am
happy to find that our principal friends have increased in

religion. Accounts from Philadelphia are pleasing – souls are converted to God. There is also a move in New York, and their numbers are daily increasing. On reviewing the labours of the last six weeks, I find we have rested about fourteen days at conferences, and ridden at least seven hundred miles.

A Christmas Present

ELLEN THORNEYCROFT FOWLER

With her first novel in 1898, Concerning Isabel Carnaby, *Wolverhampton's Ellen Thorneycroft Fowler attracted much critical acclaim. This Christmas story comes from her last published work,* Signs and Wonders, *of 1926. Her sister, Edith, was also a novelist and a Christmas extract from one of her books is given on p. 136.*

'One Christmas Eve, about ten years after my father's death, I was feeling particularly lonely and depressed. Loneliness is always a terrible complaint, and when Christmas supervenes it becomes ten times worse. I was living at the time in the hideous little new house which I hated, and my hatred of my so-called home made me feel all the more desolate.'

'It would. I always think that living in houses that you

don't like is only one degree better than living with people that you don't like.'

'I quite agree with you. I have a strong belief in the souls of houses, which you and I must fully discuss sometime. I feel sure we should think alike upon this subject, or else think quite differently, which would be just as interesting, if not more so,' replied Mrs Copeland.

'But meantime get on with your story. You'd got as far as Christmas Eve in the hideous little house.'

Thus urged, Mrs Copeland continued: 'I was helping with the Church decorations, I remember, and was feeling dreadfully envious of the other helpers who all seemed to have happy homes and cheerful family circles in which to spend their respective Christmas Days. I alone was left out in the cold. The Vicar's little daughter was aiding me in my endeavour to transform the pulpit into an ivy bush, and chattering all the time about the presents she expected on the morrow. '"My daddy is going to give me a doll's house," she said; "what is your daddy going to give you?" I explained that my father was dead, and therefore unable any longer to give Christmas presents; but as I spoke, a great wave of remembrance swept over me of the happy Christmases of long ago, when my father used always to give me the best pair of gloves that money could buy; sometimes furlined, sometimes of antelope-skin, but always with the little label stuck inside "With Father's love". Always the same present from the days of my childhood; in larger and larger sizes at first, and then sticking to six and three-quarters till they stopped altogether, and then there were no more Christmas presents for me.'

Mrs Copeland paused for a moment, and looked over the moors, and Miss Nicholls looked at her friend with sympathy in her brown eyes.

Then once more the elder lady took up her parable. 'The Vicar's little daughter looked sorry for me and suggested,

A Christmas Eve carol played by the Salvation Army

"Perhaps your daddy will send you a present down from Heaven." I vetoed the suggestion, but she still persisted: "I'll tell you what I'll do," she says: "I'll just run into the Lady Chapel and offer up a prayer for your daddy to send you a Christmas present from Heaven, the same as he used to do when he was on earth. I prayed for my doll's house, and it is coming, so if I pray for your present, I expect it will come too." I expressed grave doubts on the matter, but the dear little thing stood firm and ran into the Lady Chapel to offer up her petition on my behalf.'

'The faith of children is very simple,' remarked Miss Nicholls.

'And none the worse for that,' retorted her friend. 'I gather that unless ours is of the same brand, we shall be hard put to it at the last. Well, on Christmas morning a queer thing

happened. Just as I was starting for Church – feeling more hopelessly miserable than I had ever felt before – I found I had made my current pair of gloves so shabby at the decorations the day before, that they really were not fit to wear, so I hunted about for another pair. On the chest of drawers in my bedroom there stood an old glove-box, which I opened on the chance that there might be a pair inside. Imagine my surprise when I discovered a new pair of antelope-skin gloves, wrapped up in tissue paper, and having inside them the well-known message, "With Father's love". I could hardly believe my eyes, but there they were, and the nicest pair I think that my father had ever given me.'

'Good gracious!' exclaimed Miss Nicholls. 'However did you explain it?'

'Ah! I thought that question would come,' laughed Mrs Copeland. 'I was waiting for it. I can tell you how *you* would have explained it; you would have said that on the particular Christmas Day when my father gave me that particular pair of gloves, I wasn't needing a new pair; so I put them away till I did need them, and then forgot all about them. The old glove-box – which was a sort of standard bedroom ornament of mine – had followed me through my various removals, but I had always subconsciously regarded it as nothing but an ornament and so had never happened to open it. That is how *you* would have explained it, my dear, but I think, even you, would have been hard pressed to explain why I had not opened the glove-box for all those years, and why I did open it on Christmas morning.'

'Then how should you explain it, Mrs Copeland?' asked Janet gently.

'Oh! I should choose a far simpler and more obvious explanation; that God had heard the child's prayer and answered it, and gave me a sign that my father still loved me and remembered me on Christmas Day, as he had done when he was on

earth, and as he would go on doing to all eternity. But as to *how* God answered the prayer, I did not trouble my head; whether He used ordinary or extraordinary methods was no business of mine; it was enough for me that He had answered it, and had sent me a message which changed my whole outlook of my life, and taught me that "Like as a father pitieth his children" is no mere form of words, but a vital and glorious reality.'

A Surprise for Annie

BARBARA M. COLLINGS

A more modern tale from a female author also with Wolverhampton connections comes in this little story from a collection published as part of a creative writing project – the Bloxwich Penpushers – in the winter of 1990.

Annie pulled her woolly hat down over her ears as she walked towards the Post Office as briskly as her tired legs would allow. It was a fine crispy morning so she left the house early and decided to spend a day in Town after collecting her pension. 'It is cold enough for snow,' she thought, 'but if I hurry I will soon be in the warm shops.'

Her heart lightened as she thought of the prettily decorated shops and animated chatter of the assistants. The days up to Christmas always excited her, no doubt reminding her of the happy anticipation she had felt in her younger days when family and friends had been around to make Christmas the wonderfully happy time it was meant to be. She hurried a little faster, enthralled at the prospect of browsing amongst the shops with their pretty lights, Christmas trees and beautiful presents – far too expensive for her own pocket, but she loved looking at them and dreaming of what might have been. As she turned the corner by the Post Office, her heart sank in disbelief at the sight ahead. 'A queue! A queue! So early in the morning!' she cried in dismay, her chest heaving as visions of her day out faded fast.

Sure enough, there before her, a gigantic queue snaked out of the Post Office, past the Newsagents and the Chemists, and people from all directions were rushing to become part of the ever increasing jostling length. Annie's eyes filled with tears. 'I shall be lucky to reach the counter by mid-day,' she murmured to herself, 'So much for my day out.'

However, she patiently took her place in the queue and prepared herself for a long, slow, dismal wait in the cold. Apart from some low grumbling from the crowd, few people seemed awake enough for discourse, so Annie tried to shut out the sounds with plans for the rest of the day. Suddenly, a strident voice jerked her out of her daydream. 'Mornin' Alf! It ay a bad day is it? 'Ave yer brought yer barrer? Them payin' two weeks this mornin', we wo' arf live it up this 'oliday, wo' we?'

Alf, a small thin person, almost buried in a long old-fashioned overcoat, who was standing quietly in the queue, his capped head tucked deeply in a long striped scarf wrapped around his neck, retrieved his Pension Book from an inner pocket of his coat and groaned. 'I dunno about that Bill, I gotta pay the T.V. licence out o' this. There wo' be much left after they took that.'

'Yer wanna buy a stamp each week fer that; yer do' miss it s'much then.' Bill advised sympathetically.

'It do' go very far any time,' grumbled Alf. 'I dunno about Christmas.'

'Yer'll soon cheer up when yer've downed a pint. Yer cummin' ter the Pub at dinner time, aren't yer? Yer gotta 'ave a Christmas drink wi' us.' Bill's raucous voice sallied merrily through the sharp morning air.

'I gotta go ter the butchers fust,' Alf replied. 'See if he's got summat for nuthin.' I could just demolish one o' them fat turkeys in that there winda' but I reckon I'll 'ave ter mek do wi' a sparrer.' Alf's spirits rose as the amused crowd laughed and joined in the cheery banter.

'Yer can cum round ter me, Alf. I'll feed yer an' keep yer warm,' Old Nellie shouted, her battered felt hat slipping over one eye as she was pushed nearer the counter. 'I gorra nice bird; yer wo' starve,' she grinned cheekily.

'Yer wanna watch 'er, Alf,' Bill joked. 'Her's tryin' to find a way ter yer 'eart. Afore yer know it, she'll 'ave yer in Church.'

''er wo' arf,' Alf responded drily, 'I reckon the missus 'll 'ave summat ter say about that.'

Annie began to enjoy herself as she listened to the strange but happy exchange of conversation amongst the crowd. She didn't notice the quickly diminishing queue until miraculously she found herself at the counter.

'Do' spend it all at once ducks,' Bill bellowed, raising his trilby hat politely. ''appy Christmas to yer.'

Annie smiled back as she put her money safely in her purse. She hadn't enjoyed herself so much for a long time. It had been quite fun in the queue after all; in fact, the merry rapport had quite enriched her day. With plenty of time left and light of heart once more, she left the Post Office and hurried away to catch a bus into Town.

from

A Good Christmas Box

In 1847 a Dudley printer, George Walters, was selling for
1s 3d (6p) A Good Christmas Box *containing* A Choice
Collection of Christmas Carols. *Many of these joyous songs*
are now familiar pieces in the repertoire of many a carol singer.
This one is entitled Old Christmas Hymn.

Arise and hail the sacred day,
Cast all low cares of life away,
And thoughts of meaner things;
This day to cure our deadly woes,
The Sun of Righteousness arose,
With healing in his wings.

If angels on that happy morn,
The Saviour of the world was born,
Pour'd forth seraphic songs;
Much more should we of human race,
Adore the wonders of his grace,
To whom that grace belongs.

How wonderful, how vast his love,
Who left the shining realms above,

Those happy seats of rest!
How much for lost mankind he bore,
Their peace and pardon to restore,
Can never be exprest.

While we adore his boundless grace,
And pious mirth and joy take place,
Of sorrow, grief, and pain;
Give glory to our God on high,
And not amongst the general joy,
Forget good-will to men.

O then let heaven and earth rejoice,
Creation's whole united voice,
And hymn the happy day;
When Sin and Satan vanquish'd fell,
And all the powers of death and hell,
Before his sovereign sway.

from

The Rebels

HENRY TREECE

*A poet with a flair for writing children's historical novels set in
Roman and Viking times Henry Treece was also a prime mover
in the New Apocalypse literary movement. His short story,* Man
on the Hill, *published in 1962, describes events in 1066 from
14 October until the Christmas Day Coronation of William the
Conqueror. His second adult novel was a nineteenth-century
Darlaston family saga. In this extract Treece cannot resist a
passing reference to the Saxon mystique when describing two
brothers' Christmas confrontation in Wednesbury, the writer's
own birthplace.*

Now it was Christmas time again and the thought of the boy
came to me more and more frequently. My heart was full of a
strange yearning that I had never known before. Had I dared
go out into the town by day I would have bought a great fir
tree and dressed it up with candles and bright glass balls, to
make more tangible before my eyes the image of childhood.

I think Phyllis must have felt like this too, for after her
long silence she wrote to me, asking whether I would be able
to find the boy and bring him to her. She had ignored my letter earlier, in which I had told her of my resignation from
Griffith's Ironworks; but now as though in an excess of
Christian good-feeling she alluded to my state in her last

117

sentence, though without that warmth which might have made me take her at her word:

'Herbert asks me to tell you that he will always be willing to see you, provided that you write in advance to let him know you are coming, for as you will realise he is a much occupied man.'

I tore her letter through and dropped it on to the floor. Now my sister Phyllis was almost as much a ghost as my sister Susan. Now my family consisted only of that boy, kept from me by my stranger-enemy, Elijah Fisher. And Herbert, her staid and prosperous husband, was even less than a cypher in my mind, a disembodied spirit of tight-lipped condescension . . . I wanted none of them!

But as the time of carol-singers drew on and their young voices echoed chilly along the dark streets beyond my high wall, my mind turned again and again to the past, when we all went to church and knelt in the heavy incense-laden dimness of the pillars, to give praise to the Boy of Bethlehem; and a great desire came on me to do this thing again, once more, for the last time perhaps. My own place of worship was closed to me but there were others. I called to mind the great church on the hill at Wednesbury and there seemed to be something symbolic in my going there, an act of renunciation of my own church almost; an exercise of final rebellion.

So, shaving and changing my linen for the first time for many days, I dressed in my best dark suit and put on my formal hat and set out through the snow by back streets and side lanes towards the place I had chosen. Apart from a few children, muffled to the eyes against the bitter weather, I saw few folk out that night and I came at last to the foot of the hill almost without realising that I had already walked so far.

Above me, among the clustered houses, the church spire pointed upwards to heaven, like a gaunt burnt finger of accusation against the swirling snow. I began to make my way up

towards it, entering a curling little cobbled street, hardly more than a pathway, that mounted for a while up the slope, the guttering of the snow-covered roofs hardly higher than the crown of my hat. And after a while this narrow passage-way ended and I found myself facing a clearing, as it were, in the jungle of brickwork, the Bull Ring. Surrounded by mean dwellings on all sides, it lay like a deep granite-walled well, while the road spiralled half round it on its way up the hill, so that while on one side a man might look down thirty feet to the cobblestones of the grim place, from the other lower down the slope, his bedroom window might be placed on the same level as the ghastly rings that still dangled, circles of rusting iron, to which at one time doom-driven horned heads were chained, foam-flecked and staring, shuddering at the first onslaught of the dogs.

I stood for a moment, my coat collar turned up against the flurry of blinding snow that suddenly swept from the higher reaches of the hill over the roof-tops and across the empty place of death, into my face. And as I stood the door of one of the row of cottages that looked directly into the Bull Ring opened, throwing a broad band of orange light across the packed snow as the vicious flakes swirled heavily.

A woman came out of the cottage, a man's cap upon her head, an old black shawl about her shoulders. She stared at me blank-faced, for a matter of seconds, called back with a laugh into the room she had left and then, with a bucket in her hand, strode across the cobblestones of the ring to a pump which served all the hovels on that side of the slope.

At the first sight of her open door and its warm light, I had almost gone to the woman to ask if I might sit by her fire and warm my hands for they were numb now and aching with the cold. But there was something in the laugh which she flung back to her door like a discarded orange-peel, some contempt which put that idea from my mind.

A wintry finger has written the compliments of the season on this
bench on Lovers' Walk in Wednesbury's Brunswick Park

I began to climb the hill again, the road gradually rising
and turning until I could look down now on the woman by
the pump. She stood black below me in the snow. Her right
hand was working the pump-handle but she was looking up
at me, where I stood above her. There was not more than
twenty feet between our faces and I could hear every syllable
she said. She spoke them firmly, viciously, savouring the shape
of them on her tongue, lingering over the pauses between
them, attempting a supreme act of intimidation on me.

'Hey, yo'd better not goo up thear, Tum Fisher!' she said.
'There's them up thear 'as sworn to gi' thee an unlucky blow!'

I had no words to speak to her in answer. I just looked
down and laughed at her through the whirling snow. She
stopped pumping and hissed up at me, 'Thee cust laugh,

Fisher, but that wunna save thee, me Lord Muck, when thee brother gets 'old o' thee! Nay, that it wunna!'

Then she threw back her head and laughed up at me like some tribal hag, some dark and savage Saxon beast.

This part of the town *was* Saxon, to the last stone. It was the original fortress of Woden in these parts, where now so ironically stood the gentle church of Christ. Even the steeply-mounting steps on which my feet were now set were called Ethelfleda's Terrace, and that slattern's language, the animal vigour of the words she used, even their intonation, seemed to me ancient, of an earlier day and of a wicked dispensation; the language of such folk as mutilated the sorry British hinds who fell into their dark power. I could not bear to listen to her laughter and turned away from her up the steep hill, until at last I stopped at the top, leaning against a house wall, panting in the strong gusts that now buffeted my head.

Below me the snow spread out like a dirty table-cloth over canal towpath and railway-siding; over culvert and cupola, gantry and pit-gear; a thin cloth, through the soiled grey fabric of which protruded here the dark metals of the railway, there the long sloping ramp down which the spoil-buckets ran when they had tipped their load of useless slag. Here the dark iron-blue slates of row after row of mean houses; there the still black waters of the canals, the inland waterways on whose oily surface small bergs of ice and snow floated without purpose until their dissolution.

The night was a length of indigo serge, full of starry pinpricks and held before a fire so that the light shone through the holes where the points had pierced it. And constantly from place to place across this sky the smoky orange-red glow from furnaces rose and fell, rose and fell, like the slow pulse-beats of some monstrous volcanic heart, as here and there, in Cradley, or Tipton, or Ocker Hill, in Sedgley, or Willenhall, or Swan Village, a furnace door was opened and its bubbling

Two path-cutting operations during the heavy snows of 1947 at
opposite ends of the Black Country. Above, a way is cleared through
to the pigsties in Brandhall Lane, Warley, while below the lone
figure of Alfred Wheeler cuts a similar path into Boundary Farm at
Perton

metallic broth was exposed for a minute to the shivering snow-filled night.

I stood, staring across this harsh desert of ice and fire, no longer part of it now, able to see it for the first time for what it was, impartially, a running sulphurous sore on the green side of England. At last I was free of it, free to curse what had hitherto brought me a living; free to behave like a god sitting in judgement on Church Hill and not an outcast, a tumbled iron master, the brother of an unloving slut who had let some gipsy get her with child along a giggling canal-bank.

I began to laugh, half cynically, half hysterically, at my own sad plight, however. I was like some mineral chip that had exploded from a planet and which must wheel out in space, solitary, unattached, for ever, without hope; disowned by the iron masters, despised and jeered at by the iron workers; a lump or rock, for all eternity swinging out in space, round and round, never to know rest again.

On Church Hill three days before Christmas, I saw myself like that for the first time. I was finished, nothing more, nothing less than that. I had known this in a theatrical way before, when I was writing the letter that stood before the black marble clock in my kitchen now. But I had never known it in my bones, in my blood, in my very heart. And the full realisation of it came on me as the snow beat into my face and took my scant breath away.

Then suddenly the comic enormity of my situation burst in on me like a monstrous swishing catherine-wheel nailed to the crown of my head. I began to laugh, to roar with laughter, slapping my thighs and taking off my billy-cock so as to wipe my streaming temples!

And it was at this point, as I leaned against someone's garden wall, my laughter now turning to tears, that I heard footsteps approaching from the other side of the road. Although they were partly muffled by the heavy blanket of snow, they

were still recognisable as the steps of a man, and a definite man at that. I was in no mind to allow anyone, stranger or otherwise, to look into my face at that moment for something had happened to my spirit and I was anxious only to be left alone until such time as Tom Fisher had relearned his old courage and could face the world. I turned away from the road as though waiting for someone, but someone who would come from the opposite direction.

The footsteps came nearer. They slowed down and a voice called out, 'A Merry Christmas, mate!' Then the steps went on, leaving my heart thumping at my side, for that cheery voice was the voice of Elijah Fisher, the man, who had knocked away the last pit-prop of my happiness and let the galleries sink down upon me as I worked alone in the darkness! Then the irony of the situation came upon me so strongly that I almost laughed aloud; he, the gaolbird outcast of the family, was wishing me a Merry Christmas!

Yet how right it was that he should be the wisher and I the receiver! He seemed to have happiness and to spare, from the gay tone of his voice and the light tread of his feet. I knew now, in all truth, that I had no happiness. All I had was a sudden flaring anger that swept through my heart and head like wildfire as I listened to that firm footstep retreating away from me, safely, down the narrow winding path which I had but recently ascended, down Ethelfleda's Terrace.

I ran to the top of the slope. A jaunty little tune floated back to me, the whistling of a man who was at peace with the world, but more than that, at peace with his own heart – and the one is vastly superior to the other.

I gasped with fury and began to follow him as fast as I could on that freezing roadway. I dared not shout, for fear of betraying my intentions, for now I knew what I must do. It was fruitless to appeal to the law, which had punished my brother already at my request and without effect, and which

now had lost faith in me and might be counted on no longer to punish him. Now I must punish him myself, whatever the consequence to my future, and I was beyond considering that. No longer did my own safety mean anything to me beside my revenge. I must show him that I was head of the family still, that I was still capable of ruling somebody!

I found myself running bareheaded now, though I had not noticed the wind whip off my billycock hat, nor should I have stopped if I had noticed it for now my anger was too flood-swollen for anything to halt my mad career.

Below me on the hill, my brother moved on with a merry step, his long shadow thrown black across the snow from a street-lamp set in a bracket on one of the overhanging walls. Once I almost called out to him to stop, almost used his name; but something kept me from doing this. Perhaps it was pride, perhaps even shame, that we should share one name.

I felt my muffler come loose and work its way out of the breast of my greatcoat, and tried to push it back, but my hands were clumsy and wet and dragged it out even further when I withdrew them. I had to slow down then for the ice which was caked thickly on the cobble-stones was treacherous and more than once I almost sprawled my length upon the ground.

Now as I neared the sunken Bull Ring I saw the figure below me more clearly in the light which shone into his face from an uncurtained window. There was no doubt about his identity; there was not another nose like that in the whole of the Black Country! I clung gasping to the tall iron railings that fringed the upper lip of the Bull Ring, for my brother had stopped and was staring in through the window which illumined him, smiling and nodding and tapping on the pane with his knuckles. He was talking to someone in that little room but now the blood thudded so hard in my ears that I could not recognise his words. But suddenly I saw him feel

inside his jacket and drag out a pair of cockerels by their feet. They were gamecocks. Their heads dangled together on limp broken necks. Their gay feathers fluttered pathetically in the night wind of that Saxon hill.

Then my ears cleared and I heard his voice. 'Two o' Jacob Tranter's!' he said. 'They'll be a bit tough eatin', but no doubt they'll make a drop o' good broth for the bairn! Yo' c'n come, and welcome, if yo'd like a bit o' chicken! But yo'll 'a to file yer teeth, no doubt!'

Then he had waved and gone on further down the hill, away from the light, into the thick and driving snow, towards the row of squalid cottages situated on the lower edge of the Ring.

I was suddenly afraid of losing him now in the blinding flurry and began to run as fast as I dared, almost praying that I might catch up with him before the darkness wrapped him away from me.

But without warning there came a most vicious fluster of snow, a small but intense blizzard, which struck my bare head with so sudden a blow that one of my legs caught against the other and came near to upsetting me. I spun round, my mouth wide open for breath, my eyes shut tight against the sharp and painful crystals that had blown against them. I groped out and found the railings once more and hung on to them until the vice had gone out of the storm.

Immediately below me the snowflakes swirled round and round in the Bull Ring like some horrid Polar broth being stirred; then across the broad space, I saw a door open and then close again, its ochreous light being cut off almost as soon as it had appeared. I felt certain that my brother had entered that cottage, out of the storm. That house must be the haven of his villainy. So, without intending to, I had tracked down Elijah Fisher. Now we should see who had the right to the child, Susan's boy, my boy!

I loosed the railings and ran the rest of the way down the curving slope, skirting the Bull Ring and coming up before the row of squat hovels. They lay like hunched and snarling beasts, well below the level of the pavement, so that one looked down through their lower windows, and might almost reach up to clasp the sill of their upper ones. I ran the length of the row, staring down through their windows, yet did not catch a glimpse of my brother. These windows were shielded, or half-shielded, by old rags, torn garments, newspapers or strips of cardboard, one even by an ancient umbrella, the ribs of which protruded like the bones of a creature rotting in a desert. Yet in each of these kennels burned candle or lamp or tallow-dip, as though their inhabitants were celebrating their meagre Christmas as brightly as they could by their poverty-striken lights.

I knew that Elijah Fisher was there, in one room or another and that where he was the child, my child, would be found too. I had come too far now to abandon my search.

Never in my life had I so abased myself as to knock on such doors as these to ask a favour. Now I felt that I should be acting like a beggar, a thing of damnation, if I were to rap on that blistered, splintering wood and then stand meekly until someone should choose to answer the door and deign to tell me whether Elijah Fisher and his two dead gamecocks were within. A violent wave of nausea swept over me, filling my head, swamping my faculty of reason, I think. I was damned if I would go cringing like a puppy dog to find my brother. No, I would visit these stinking cottages like the wrath of God, and they should know my force at last. They should know what it was to scorn Tom Fisher!

I heard myself laugh then, a brittle high-pitched laugh that came to my ears more like the hysterical cackling of a drunken street-woman than the raging fury of a ruined man. I felt that I had to run from that laugh now, to escape from its

weakness, somehow or other, for to me as I stood there the echoing sound of that pathetic noise was an admission of my failure, my hopeless failure in a life that had once seemed so secure. And I had to run from that failure, come what may. 'Damn him! Let me find him, and then . . .' I said, as I ran down the narrow brick steps to the cottage.

'Come out, Fisher,' I shouted then and grasped at the latch of the door. It did not give way to me immediately and I flung the weight of my body against it. The flimsy door gave

'The jungle of brickwork surrounded by mean dwellings on all sides'

and I stumbled into the single-roomed hovel, only to pull myself up with a bewildered jolt when I had done so. The room was dim and full of shadows, being lighted only by a small tallow-wick that floated in a saucer on the dusty ledge of the window. The uneven earthen floor on which my feet slithered was thick with neglected refuse and the foetid air damp with the steam that issued forth constantly and vehemently from a great iron kettle, set among the glowing coals of a narrow rusting fireplace. So heavy was the place with moisture that I could scarcely breathe, yet as my eyes became accustomed to the gloom, I saw that the kettle served a humane purpose.

Fighting for her breath, on a couch made of sacks and packing-wood and half-covered with filthy rags, lay a haggard-faced young girl of fourteen or so. Her long black hair lay tangled about her head, on which the beads of sweat stood like ghastly pearls. Her blue and heavy-lidded eyes opened with alarm as I staggered towards her through the steam and she tried to rise, holding up a thin arm as though to shield her face.

'Nay, dunna hit me again, Dadda,' she said in fear. 'I couldn't help it. I couldn't help it, I was cold! Dunna tak yer belt off, Dadda!'

Then she began to sob, plucking at the tattered coverlet, senselessly, rhythmically, as though there was no heart left to break but only an eternal rehearsing of the breaking-scene.

My own anger fell away from me like a discarded garment. Now I was torn by another emotion, stronger for a moment even than the one which had brought me to this place. I would have gone to her, to comfort her in some dumb unknown way. My hands were already outstretched towards her when I was taken from behind by the collar of my coat and swung round. The doorway seemed crowded with the faces of people, vicious sneering faces. The man who bundled

me from the door and up the narrow steps outside was shouting in my ear, 'I wunna 'a thee touch 'er! Thy hand shall never touch my lass, Tum Fisher!'

I could still hear the sick girl's crying from the open door, as plaintive in that night as the cry of a lamb. Then they spun me round and I stood swaying in the whistling snow, dizzy with surprise, my enemies in a half-circle about me, men and women and even children, jeering and cursing and snarling like beasts from some mean and sulphurous jungle.

Then someone yelled out, 'I towd thee not to come up 'ere, Tum Fisher! I warned thee they'd gi' thee a bad blow, thee saft owd fool!' It was the woman in the man's cap. She held a poker in her hand and came forward to me threateningly. The others followed her, jeering, the children snatching up handfuls of snow and garbage and flinging them in my face. I backed before them, holding up my arms to protect myself as the creature lunged towards me.

Then with the savage hooting of their laughter in my ears, I felt cobblestones beneath my feet, sensed high granite walls about me and I realised that I was penned in the old Bull Ring, to be baited as these hooligans chose.

My first impulse was to break through them, to show them that they had corned a bull this time and not a rat. But even as I moved forward with a shout, a great man wearing a dirty open shirt and the moleskins of a furnaceman, swung his leather belt in my face. The heavy brass buckle took me across the temples and I slipped on the cobbles, losing my balance for the moment. While I staggered, a young girl who wore the bright ear-rings and gaudy neck-cloth of a gipsy, pushed out at me with both her hands, laughing as she did so. I fell back against the wall. I could retreat no farther now!

Then they were on me, kicking at my legs, clutching at my collar, dragging down at my coat. The woman in the cap struck out with her poker, a blow meant for my head but

which glanced across the bone of my shoulder, paralysing my arm for the moment.

Now, after my first roar and their first gibes, we fought silently in the snow as animals might, gasping and grunting for breath, striking out and kicking wherever there was room to move hand or foot. Once I was down and for a while a great terror plunged over me as I thought they would stifle me in the slush. Then just as suddenly I was on my feet again, hanging on to something, something cold and metallic. It was an iron ring set in the wall, a ring which they had once chained the other bellowing creatures whom they would torment.

Yet as I clung there like a spent swimmer, the man with the leather belt struck again with all his strength, coldly, taking careful aim. Half-blinded I fell, still grasping the ring

Deanery Row, Wolverhampton, 1955

which my weight must have dragged from its crumbled socket, tasting the warm blood which ran into the corner of my mouth, lying in the trampled muddy snow, now scarce able to breathe for the insane galloping of my heart.

For a while there was a dreadful silence through which I heard a woman's voice call, 'Thou'st done it now, Jabez Cutler! That thou hast and no mistake!' And someone else, perhaps the gipsy-girl, laughed out loud, shrilly and without humour.

Then as in the confused uproar of waters I heard many things; I heard the trailing echo of that hysterical laugh; my own painful gasp that turned surprisingly into a roar of fury, as I found myself rising without willing to do so, the new iron weapon in my hand; but above all other sounds, the voice of my brother, Elijah, riding abreast the snow-filled winds like an eagle sweeping into battle.

'Stand off, you coward bastards! Is this the way to carry on when a man's back's turned! Let him be, you scum, or I'll break your filthy necks!'

I was on my feet now, arms dangling at my side, my right hand painful from gripping the iron ring with such force. My tormentors fell back before me like hounds before a stag. And beyond them the tall spare figure of my brother towered above them all. Now I had forgotten them and I remembered only the man who had brought me to this sorry state. And I went towards him, my temples banging with blood, nursing my last ounce of strength to strike him down.

The crowd saw my eyes and fell back around me so that Elijah and I stood alone in the open ring.

'I am coming for thee, Elijah Fisher!' I said, raising my hand to strike. 'Now the score will be even!'

I saw him above me, standing stock-still as my hand came down. He seemed to be without the power to move. The ring caught him on the cheek, and I struck again and again. And each time he seemed to grow taller and taller until he towered

over me, smiling down at me kindly as though I was caressing him and not killing him.

Then I felt his arms round me, raising me up, and he was saying, 'Poor Tom; poor lad! They've knocked thee about, owd chap! If I'd been 'ere they'd not done this!'

And his eyes were soft and gentle as they looked down into mine, and his hands were soft and gentle, like those of a young mother to her first child. And he lifted me up as though I was as light as a young girl and began to carry me away across the Bull Ring through the snow. And I knew that they were all following us meekly, like curs that have done wrong and now are afraid. The fury had drained from me with my strength. Now at last I knew that my brother was a stronger man than I was, a better man, and I began to weep in my defeated weakness, without shame, without any wish to hide my face, a child again, in my father's arms, fearing him and yet loving him at the same time.

So before my senses left me utterly, I lay by a kitchen fire in one of the cottages, side by side with a little child in its cradle. Elijah bent over me and said, 'What is it, our Tum? What do you want, lad?'

And I said, 'Is that the child, her child?'

He nodded and smiled strangely. 'It was her child, but now it's mine. Mine and thine, brother, if we can learn the way to live together in peace again.'

I took his hand in mine and said, so weakly that he had to bend his head over me to hear my words, 'We have been enemies too long, 'Lijah. Now I'm too far gone to fight thee any longer, lad. All I have in the world is the lad's, tell him one day. That's all I have to say.'

Elijah looked down at me and touched me on the face. 'Let us go away, our Tun,' he said. 'Away from 'ere where they all know us. Let us tak the bairn and go to our Phyllis's! There's some job I can do, never fear. We'll get a trap as soon as thee canst travel, and we'll go together. What dost say, our kid?'

Now it seemed to me that I suffered more terribly than I had done in the Bull Ring. Then they only hurt my pride and my body; now it was my very spirit that was being wrenched from its sockets.

I grasped my brother's hands. 'It is the thing I want most in the world,' I said. 'It will be the lion-coloured days come again, our kid!'

Then the hot tears spurted from his eyes and ran down my face, and I smiled at him and went to sleep even before my mouth had finished smiling.

from

A Second Dudley Book of Cookery

GEORGINA, COUNTESS OF DUDLEY

In 1909 the then Dowager Countess of Dudley published her Dudley Book of Cookery and Household Recipes *which proved a popular seller. In this later work her ladyship gives various recipes for turkey in the poultry and game category but this particular extract comes from the miscellaneous section.*

AN EXCELLENT OLD-FASHIONED RECIPE FOR MINCEMEAT FOR CHRISTMAS MINCE PIES

One pound of stoned raisins, one pound of clean, picked sultanas, one pound of currants, a quarter of a pound of mixed peel, one tablespoonful of mixed spice, one pound of apples peeled and cut into pieces, one pound of castor sugar, three lemons and three oranges (the grated rind and juice), two pounds of lean, cooked fillet of beef, free from fat, one pound of very finely chopped beef suet, one pint of cooking brandy and one pint of rum.

Pass twice through a mincing machine the raisins, peel, sultanas, apples and beef, to make it very fine. Place this in a large bowl; add the currants, sugar, spice, chopped suet, orange and lemon rind and juice; wet it with the wine; mix all well together and place in jars for about four weeks before using.

This will keep for months in a cool place if well tied down to keep the air from it.

Dudley Castle gateway

Christmas

EDITH HENRIETTA FOWLER

*Sister of novelist Ellen Thorneycroft Fowler (see p. 108), Edith
also wrote a number of books, including the children's novel*
The Young Pretenders. *Its delightful description of
Christmas is retold here. For her own children she dedicated the
biography of their grandfather, Viscount Wolverhampton, one-
time government minister, who was previously mayor and
Member of Parliament for Wolverhampton.*

'Do take me, Charley! I want so dreadfully to go, and it will
be an awful disappointment to me if you won't.'

Uncle Charley was just going to refuse his wife's request
when he remembered Babs's generosity:

'I would not like her to be at all 'pointed, you see.' Baby
consideration, but it influenced his decision and won Aunt
Eleanor's cause.

'I will go for the dance, then,' said Charley Conway slowly,
'and we will come back to town on Christmas Day, and have
the children down to late dinner, and a Christmas tree in the
afternoon.' With which Aunt Eleanor had to be content.

So Uncle Charley had a lovely Christmas tree made in
secret; and the children crept out of bed and hung up their
stockings on Christmas Eve, after their usual happy custom.

Babs could not sleep very well for the excitement of Santa
Claus and his nocturnal visit, so she jumped out of bed very

The turn on Compton Holloway

early and felt for the enriched stocking. There it hung, hollow and limp as on the night before.

'Oh, Teddy!' she almost groaned, stealing into his room, 'Santa Claus has forgot.'

'Forgot what?' asked Teddy sleepily.

'Christmas! And the stockings is kite empty!' cried Babs in an anguish of disappointment.

The awful news banished sleep from Teddy's blue eyes, and the children sat together on the bed sorrowfully regarding the two empty black stockings with a woe almost too deep for words, till nurse came in with the unpleasant information that they were catching their deaths of cold.

Breakfast was very serious that morning, and Babs's bread-and-milk proved unusually choky.

The little girl sadly laid the needle-case on nurse's plate,

and then nurse gave the children each a china mug with 'Be good' stamped on in gold letters.

'Do you like the mugs, Teddy?' asked Babs when they were alone together.

'No,' answered her brother crossly, 'I think they're horrid.'

'I fink they will make drinking rather too scolding,' continued Babs, ''cause that big "Be good" 'minds me so much of nurse when she speaks scolding.'

'You ought to remember people by their presents,' said Teddy.

'I know! "When this you see, remember me," Mrs Forrester always wrote in her presents. But I fink I'd rather forget nurse, wouldn't you, Teddy?'

'Yes, I would, and I hate her old presents!'

'Oh, Teddy, I fink it would be naughty and rather rude to hate them; but still I do wish that they hadn't been kite such stern mugs.'

'Hullo, children! Where are you?' shouted Uncle Charley directly he came home. 'A merry Christmas to you!'

'Oh! Uncle Charley!' screamed Babs, rushing into his arms, 'we aren't a bit merry, 'cause Santa Claus kite forgot our stockings.'

'What an idiot I am!' exclaimed Uncle Charley, who saw that his elaborate Christmas preparations had fallen so short of the mark; and then to the children:

'It is all right, youngsters! Santa Claus left me his presents for a Christmas tree this afternoon; a splendid big jolly one,' he added, smiling at the sudden change in their faces. 'So we will have a merry Christmas after all!'

'Oh, yes,' laughed Babs, 'I'se so glad you've come home, 'cause you make fings all right again.'

And it really was a beautiful tree, all covered with tiny coloured candles and hung with the loveliest presents; just the very things the children most wanted.

There was only one cloud. Aunt Eleanor gave Teddy and Babs a little tricycle between them. A very handsome present, but their aunt did not know the anguish of a shared possession.

'Betweens aren't never nobody's real own,' complained Babs afterwards; and the very wheels of that dainty little machine seemed always weighed by the burdensome thought that it was not the rider's very own.

'One's very own,' is a mystic charm of childhood that lends lustre even to a discarded pen-wiper, or any treasure of the waste-paper basket and rag-bag.

And when the tree was stripped of its miscellaneous fruit, there was the excitement of giving Uncle Charley his present.

'Guess once more afore you open it,' said Babs holding out the little parcel, soiled through much handling.

The premises of Penn's cab and car proprietor seen here in a winter of the 1890s

Uncle Charley felt it carefully while the children shrieked with laughter.

'I guess an ink-pot,' he said at last.

Babs clapped her hands.

'Now open it!' she screamed.

And there lay a big, wooden, tartan-painted *serviette* ring.

'Isn't it lovely!' exclaimed Babs proudly. 'The plaid 'minded me so much of Giles's Sunday pocket-handkerchief. And it'll be so useful 'cause you can have it every day at lunch and dinner.'

Uncle Charley kissed his thanks, and seemed so pleased that the children were delighted. And even Aunt Eleanor laughed a little too, and thanked Babs quite kindly for the matchbox.

'Here, Parker,' said Captain Conway to the butler, 'be sure and put this at my place at dinner tonight, and at lunch too.'

'Oh, Charley!' interrupted Aunt Eleanor, as the children rushed off to superintend the laying of the table, 'not at lunch tomorrow, the Hartlands are coming and it is too awfully vulgar.'

'Yes, it is too awfully vulgar!' repeated her husband in a curious voice. He was not referring to Babs's taste in the wooden ring, but his wife's hopeless want of taste – in her incapability of ever seeing the deeper thing.

Christmas Day in West Bromwich Workhouse

BY ONE WHO WAS THERE

The public conception of Christmas Day in the workhouse stems from the popular piece of parlour poetry by George R. Sims. Despite today's state and personal pensions there are still family memories of the anxiety and dread of ending up in the workhouse. This description, however, tries to portray even a workhouse Christmas as a cheerful affair. It comes from a local newspaper of 1904.

At bugle call on Christmas morning I woke with the thought, 'How shall I spend today?' It was soon evident to me that great preparations had been in progress for making this Workhouse bright and cheerful to the 820 persons within its walls. There may linger in some minds the old notion that to enter the 'House' means to be harshly dealt with, but to me and many others situated as I am such notions have long ago been dispelled. I dressed, listening to the strains of that glorious Christmas hymn, 'Hark, the Herald Angels sing'. At first I thought it was being sung by some voluntary choir, but I afterwards found that a thoughtful official had been brightening

us up with this song on his own gramaphone. Thank him! a good start. Breakfast (which I found was the ordinary Sunday breakfast) was served in a well-lighted, decorated Dining Hall. Then followed a well-attended Christmas morning service, conducted by the Chaplain – bright, cheerful, not too long – just the thing needed for us poor fellows, and then I saw quick time movements to prepare the Dining Hall for Christmas dinner. They knew how to serve a dinner, for in about fifteen minutes 250 of us had been carved for from some well-cooked roast beef, vegetables served, ale and mineral waters supplied, and we all fell to in down-right earnest. Soon steaming plum pudding followed. Some of us tried a bit, but nearly all reserved this 'tit bit' for another day. Oranges for dessert, then a quiet pipe and chat or a saunter round the yard filled in the rest of the afternoon. I noticed that each woman was presented with a packet, which I was told contained tea and sugar, so I expect that they had a quiet talk over their afternoon tea. Supper was served in the same room, consisting of the ordinary Sunday evening meal. An evening service followed, then eight bells sounded – off to bed, lights out – and it was then that I was able to look back upon a Christmas day happily spent even in a Workhouse. Monday morning I heard that the inmates were making up a programme for an entertainment in the evening. I was half inclined to ask the old stagers who prepared the list to put me down for a speech, but eventually I stuck to my first resolve not to let my name appear. However, I went to the entertainment, the Master presided, the inmates were heartily applauded, the officials helped to entertain – two in a remarkably good get-up did the cake walk well, and also sung, 'Won't you come home, Bill Bailey'. Bill has come home, I am told, and is now in the Workhouse. I also heard a good record on the gramaphone obtained by one of the officials from inmates in one of the wards at the Workhouse, and which was wonderfully well done. Punctually at eight o'clock the Master

The sister and nurses starchily ready in the dining hall of Walsall's
workhouse at Christmas 1910

dismissed us to our wards, and I must acknowledge that I
had spent a 'Happy Christmas'. The visitors included the
Mayor, Mayoress, and family, Messrs G. Jewell and A.A.
James, Councillor Chesshire, Miss Chesshire, and Mr J.
Chesshire, jun.

The Master of the Workhouse reports the following gifts: A
Christmas letter to each inmate, Miss Lloyd, Sparkbrook,
Birmingham; illustrated texts, Mrs John Drew, Wellington
Road, Handsworth; evergreens, Mr S. Woodhall, 'Ivy Dene',
Great Barr; bon-bons, crackers, and new pennies to children,
Mr Councillor Chesshire; oranges, Messrs Probert, Williams,
and Co.; toys, Dr A.S. Underhill, Dr B.C. Scott, indoor staff
Chief Offices Prudential Assurance Company, London; scrap
books, the Misses Smallman, Silverdale, West Bromwich;

periodicals, Miss Langford, 34, Crocketts Road, Handsworth; Mr C. Couse, High Street, West Bromwich; Mr A. Sara, 108, Holyhead Road, Handsworth; Mrs W. Withers, 1, Bagnall Street, West Bromwich; Mrs Weston, West Smethwick; packets of tea, sugar, and tobacco, Miss Salter and Miss Savory, Springfields, West Bromwich; 10s. for Catholic inmates from Wednesbury, from Mr I. Lacey, Bilston Road, Wednesbury; £10, *Free Press* Children's Penny Benevolent Fund.

> *An article in* The Blackcountryman *by J. Godfrey describes the slightly more liberal regime found at the Wordsley workhouse which offered a greater variety of Christmas fare and ignored the usual eight-o'clock-to-bed rule. (In another report, the West Bromwich women were allowed the choice of tobacco or tea and sugar, unlike their Wordsley counterparts, who were only offered some sweets.)*

Christmas was the very special time of year, for although the meals were served at the same times as any other day, there was an ample supply of good things for everyone, with no restriction on the quantity. The day would start well with bacon and sausages for breakfast, but the main event was dinner when the menu would consist of roast beef and home-fed roast pork, roast potatoes, parsnips and brussels sprouts, followed by plum pudding and mince pies. There would be beer to drink, with mineral water for the very few who preferred it. Finally a clay pipe and tobacco for the men, and since at this time cigarettes were not the done thing for ladies, the women all had some sweets. The Chairman of the Board and local guardians visited during dinner time, and after tea the tables were cleared away and a concert would be given by nurses and other staff and various local talent. If the bell did ring on Christmas night it was ignored, and it would be late when everyone retired for the night.

from

Tiger Lilies

JUDITH GLOVER

*A Christmas party for the children of the employees of
Wolverhampton stores owner George Dennison provides an
opportunity for the first encounter between his own daughter
and that of his mistress. Romantic novelist Judith Glover uses
pre-First World War Wolverhampton as a setting for the start
of her sixth novel.*

In the end there were more than fifty children invited to the
Christmas party, and Dennison's Stores hired a church hall in
Wolverhampton to accommodate them all. Thank goodness the
weather was fine; cold, but with a brittle, bright December sun
pouring in at the windows to add its illusion of warmth to the
two Dutch stoves burning cheerfully at either end of the hall.

The sober drabness of the place, redolent of soup-kitchen
evangelism, had been entirely transformed by the gaiety of
festive decorations. Swags of paper chains festooned the wood-
en rafters, filling the space overhead with a kaleidoscope of
colour; there were bunches of holly looped with red ribbon
against the plainness of the walls; and best of all, a splendid
Christmas tree bedecked with glittering tinsel and shining
glass baubles, and hung from the lower boughs with presents,
each of which bore the name of one of the young guests here
this afternoon.

145

The wrapping and labelling of the presents had been Flora's responsibility.

First of all, while everyone was settling down and to get them into the right, jolly mood, a sing-song was conducted by one of the store managers dressed as a clown. The programme contained a medley of nursery rhymes and carols and favourite seasonal tunes and – most popular by far – the patter-songs of music hall turns, learned at home from parents; but after a while of this, small throats began to get thirsty and heads to turn longingly towards the trestle tables laid out ready at the other end of the hall.

One of Flora's suggestions for this party was that every child should be given a number as he or she came in, matching a corresponding one on the table settings. She had even gone as far as cutting out coloured circles of cardboard with the numbers boldly crayoned on, to be affixed to the recipient's garment with a safety-pin. George Dennison had thought this a capital method of avoiding what he called 'a free-for-all bunfight at teatime' and praised his young daughter accordingly; and it gave Flora a glow of achievement now to look round the noisy, crowded hall at this mixed assembly of children, all sporting one of her numbered circles like a badge of identity.

Her eyes stopped at a girl in an ivory-coloured muslin frock with deep lace collar and satin sash, standing against the wall at the back. Expecting to see her here, she knew at once who it was; but even so the sight of Roseen O'Connor made Flora catch her breath with sudden sharpness, as though startled. She stared at her, watched her joining in the singing, animated and confident, hands on hips, tapping time with one foot; and wondered whether they'd be seated near one another at tea, close enough to speak. And then, later, she didn't know whether to feel relieved or disappointed when she found herself sitting directly opposite the girl, but at a separate table.

Roseen had obviously recognised her too. From time to
time she glanced across from her place, unsmiling, something
almost spiteful in the way her expression narrowed slightly.
Then she would turn away again to her neighbour, a nice-
looking boy who kept catching Flora's eye and winking; and
the laughter would spring back into Roseen's face and the
sunny exuberance of her manner spill over everyone round her.

Her attractiveness fascinated Flora. Spellbound her. It con-
jured up in her mind instant images of the enchanted damsels
of Mr Lang's fairy tales. The heroines with whom she filled
her adolescent dreams were beautiful and lithe and noble,
with hair of just that shade of Roseen's copper-gold, rippling
in waves about their shoulders. She was reminded of Fair
Olwen, and Imogen, and the Countess of the Fountains. What
a pity the two of them could not be chums! Why did the girl
appear so to dislike her? Perhaps she should ask, and find out
. . . if only she weren't so ridiculously shy.

As a matter of fact it was Roseen herself who broke the ice
and – typically – was first to sound an overture of friendship.
Her mother Connie had threatened her to be on her best
behaviour at the Dennison's Stores party; no showing-off, no
pushing and shoving for food, no fighting, and most of all, *no*
mentioning Uncle George. She'd have to pretend she didn't
know him hardly. Never mind why. Just do as she was told if
she knew what was good for her.

Knowing what was good for her was something Roseen had
learnt early in life, and so she had paid no attention to her
Uncle George this afternoon, apart from saying hallo and
smiling when he'd winked. She was inclined not to pay any
attention to his daughter either, no matter how much the
silly, fat thing gawped and goggled every time she looked in
her direction. But a little voice of native cunning whispered
she'd do better for herself to make friends with Flora
Dennison than keep on ignoring her. What had she to lose,

A post-Christmas party given by Marsh & Baxter of Brierley Hill in
January 1963

after all? It could work out to her advantage – her Uncle
George would be pleased, she was sure. She might even get an
invitation to stay at Stockwell End with them.

And so she'd put on her sweetest and most beguiling smile
and gone across the hall to speak to Flora.

After tea was ended and the tables cleared away, and those
who wished or needed to had visited the lavatory outside, the
young guests were entertained by a professional magician
complete with silk top hat, magic wand and a black cloak big
enough to wrap round him twice. He began with a few simple
tricks, plucking fans of cards seemingly out of thin air, and
then, to the ohs and crikeys of his enraptured audience, went
on to produce an astonishing number of different objects from
various parts of his person. Coloured handkerchiefs appeared

from his wax-mustachio'd mouth, drawn out in an endless line, all knotted together like naval flags on a halyard; white mice ran from a coat sleeve shown to be empty of everything except its owner's arm; rabbits popped from the hat he'd just swept from his head in a bow; and the cloak revealed all kinds of wonders, from torn-out patterns to real live pigeons which flew up with a clap of wings and settled themselves among the decorated rafters.

'I've seen him before,' Roseen said, coming and leaning on the back of Flora's chair. 'He was at the Empire Palace.'

The other girl turned and looked up; and when she saw who it was there, a blush of confusion spread across her cheeks in a quick stain of colour. For some silly reason, to find herself suddenly so close to Roseen O'Connor made her bashful, and to her mortification all she could answer was, 'Oh . . . his name is Mr Williams, but he calls himself Maurice the Magnifico.'

'He was billed as something else when I saw him,' Roseen said, kneeling down at Flora's side and resting her arm in the most natural way on the other's knee. 'He's good, though. He sawed a woman completely in half, right through her middle.'

'Right through her – ?' Flora was horrified. 'Heavens, but didn't that hurt her?'

'Go on, it was only a trick!'

What a juggins, Roseen told herself; fancy believing a thing like that. Aloud she went on, stroking the soft material of Flora's party frock, 'I do like this you're wearing. It's ever so pretty. Your Dad buy it you, did he?'

'Well – actually – my mother's dressmaker made it specially.' A shy smile pressed dimples into Flora's cheeks. 'Yours is pretty too.'

'This old thing? No it in't. I hate it.'

Roseen pulled her hand of friendship away and a sullen little pout threatened to betray the quick resentment. It wasn't

fair. Herself, she'd had to make do with a frock bought off the landlady of the White Rose, whose daughter had outgrown it. There'd been quite a shindy at home. She didn't want anybody else's second-hand stuff! Uncle George would buy her a frock for the party if she asked him. But Connie had put her foot down. She wasn't to expect Uncle George to go reaching in his pocket for every blessed thing she wanted. Folk didn't like being taken for granted. About time she learned that.

'Your name's Roseen, isn't it,' Flora said above the sound of applause for Maurice the Magnifico. 'I'm Flora – Flora Dennison. We've seen each other before, if you remember.'

'Have we?'

'Yes. A long time ago, though. My Papa brought me to Raby Street once, and called at your house.'

Roseen tossed the ringlets from her shoulders and made no answer, pretending to give her attention to the magician's next trick.

'You were looking out from an upstairs window. You waved goodbye as he left.'

There was a half-shrug. She recalled the occasion very well. She also recalled feeling bitterly jealous of the well-dressed child queening it below in Uncle George's pony trap.

'No, I don't remember,' she said. Then, suddenly, distracted by something and switching again to her most winning manner, 'Here, are all those presents on the Christmas tree for us lot?'

'The presents – ? Oh, yes. Yes, they are. They're to be given out at the end of the party, just before everyone leaves.'

A happy thought struck Flora, and she went on in a quick rush, 'I say, you wouldn't like to help, would you? I'm supposed to be the one giving the presents, you see, and . . . well . . . it would be jolly nice if you'd lend me a hand.'

Jolly nice. Roseen squirmed inside with laughter.

''Course I'll help, if you want,' she answered, leaning her-

self back once more and resting her head against the other's arm as though in a spontaneous gesture of girlish affection.

Her hair in its bandeau of cream satin ribbon brushed Flora's hand. She longed to reach out and stroke the red-gold softness. Shyly she said instead, 'I'd like you to be my friend, Roseen. Will you? Please?'

She couldn't see the bitter-sweet expression, half triumph, half contempt, which touched those smiling lips.

Acknowledgements

The extract from *Ruffy and Sons* by George Woden, published by Hutchinson Books Ltd in 1945 is reprinted with acknowledgement to the copyright holder of the author, George Wilson Slaney. *The Carol of the Fir-Tree* by Alfred Noyes is reproduced by kind permission of Mr Hugh Noyes. The extracts from *Nurse on Call* by Edith Cotterill, published in 1986 by Century Hutchinson Ltd, are reproduced with permission from the Random Century Group. 'Christmas Eve' is from *Secret Stepmother* by Alice Lunt, published by J.M. Dent & Sons Ltd, and is reproduced by kind permission of the copyright holder, Miss Hilda Hunter. The extract from *Bilston Wesleyan Methodism* by John Freeman is reproduced with kind permission from Bilston Methodist Church. 'Black Country Pantomime' by Charles Hatton was included in *Black Country Folk* published by Cornish Brothers Ltd and is reproduced with acknowledgement to the original publishers, The Birmingham Post & Mail Ltd. 'Christmas Memories' by Pat Warner is reproduced from *Lock Keeper's Daughter* with kind permission from the latest printing of 1990 by Shepperton Swan Ltd, The Clock House, Upper Halliford, Shepperton, Middlesex. The extract from *Portrait of Clare* by Francis Brett Young, published by William Heinemann Ltd, is reproduced by permission of the copyright holder. The extract from *The Journal of Francis Asbury* is reproduced by the kind permission of the Editorial Committee of Epworth Press. 'A

Surprise for Annie' by Barbara M. Collings is from *Queue Lines: the Bloxwich Book of Queues* and is reproduced by kind permission of the author. The extract from *The Rebels* by Henry Treece, published by Victor Gollancz Ltd, 1953, is reproduced by permission of © The Estate of Henry Treece. The extract from an article, 'Memories of Wordsley Hospital 1913–1954', by J. Godfrey, is reproduced from *The Blackcountryman* by kind permission of the editor. The extract from *Tiger Lilies* by Judith Glover is reproduced by permission of the publishers, Hodder & Stoughton Ltd. Many thanks are offered to all those publishers and literary organizations for their assistance in tracing copyright holders.

The compiler would like to express his thanks to the archives and local studies staff in each of the four Black Country Metropolitan Boroughs (Dudley, Sandwell, Walsall, and Wolverhampton) for all their help and advice. Thanks are also due to staff at Birmingham Libraries, Glasgow Libraries, and Wolverhampton Art Gallery. A special word of thanks to Frank Power of Dudley for all his help with the selection and reproduction of photographs.

Picture Credits